CHANGING
THE NUMBERS

HOW TO DELIVER ADVISORY
SERVICES FOR MAXIMUM SUCCESS

DELLA HUDSON FCA

Changing the Numbers

Copyright Della Hudson © 2022

ISBN 978-1-913713-90-4

First Published by Compass-Publishing UK 2022
www.compass-publishing.com

Printed in the United Kingdom

A catalogue version of the book can be found at the British Library

Designed by The Book Refinery Ltd
www.thebookrefinery.com

CONTENTS

CONTENTS

CONTENTS

Part 2 - What advisory services to provide - 97

CONTENTS

CONTENTS

Foreword

"Compliance is dead; long live advisory!" they said.

But that hasn't quite turned out to be true.

Advisory hasn't been the magic bullet that has brought tremendous value to clients and tremendous wealth to the firms who deliver it. In fact, for many firms, work seems as hard as ever, they feel valued less and they aren't getting the financial rewards they hoped they would; this has never been highlighted more than through what we saw during the pandemic.

I'm in the privileged position of being able to have very intimate conversations with senior leaders across a range of accounting businesses, from the top 50 right down to armies of one, so I get to see what's really happening – and what's not.

The firms who believed the myth that "Compliance is dead; long live advisory!" really struggled. I know of firms who were using payroll as a loss-leader; were breaking even on compliance services, bookkeeping and software; and were making all of their profit from advisory services.

Then what happened? Covid-19 hit, and businesses panicked.

They scaled back on more longer-term advisory services.

They needed more advice on their tax position and compliance services.

And payroll became the hottest topic ever, requiring enormous focus and effort from the firms who served them, with a word no one had ever uttered before appearing in nearly every sentence: furlough.

So, the services that made the money were scaled back, and the effort required to deliver the services that made the least was being ramped up, putting firms in a very vulnerable position, and highlighting the fragility of this model and the thinking that underpinned it.

The reason these firms struggled was that they believed the hype, they failed to create a consistently profitable accounting business across all their services, and they failed to recognise the incredible value they bring to everything they do.

The truth is that the really successful accounting businesses put their clients as their North Star beneath which they build a sturdy foundation of services that bring huge value in their own right, and even more value as a collective. They create great breadth and depth in their service offerings, on which their clients can develop successful businesses or achieve greater personal wealth, and are thus freed up to focus on the activities that are most important to them.

In this model, where each service is profitable and stands on its own two feet; where none represents a Jenga brick that, if removed, would bring the whole house down; and where each service contributes to the financial maturity and success of the client – in that model, providing advisory services does become extremely valuable and worthwhile.

They give clients insights that they're never had before.

They enable them to make considered decisions in a timely fashion – based on data, not on their gut.

They empower clients to set clear goals to reach for and to know what dials need to be turned in order to stay on track towards those goals.

Ultimately, they help people – mums and dads and individuals, with hopes and dreams and fears – to live more fulfilled lives by reaching their financial targets, through which they find freedom and happiness.

And that's why we do what we do.

Accounting will always be a heart-centred business that impacts people and changes lives. That's what makes it so exciting.

Advisory services, if done in the right way, put you firmly in the seat next to the client as a marine co-pilot, helping them to steer their ship more successfully. But knowing if providing advisory services is right for you, which ones to choose, how to provide them, how to sell them, how to communicate their value, how to price them for success and how they fit in with the rest of the suite of services you provide is critical to your and your clients' success.

Compliance isn't dead, and neither does advisory have all the answers.

We must take a step back and make careful and considered decisions around this if we are to avoid exposing ourselves to unnecessary vulnerabilities, to provide the most value we possibly can and to be richly rewarded as a result.

Throughout this book, Della does a stellar job of getting accounting businesses to take that considered step back and to understand fully what the right direction is for them. Della has been tremendously generous in bringing her years of experience from building and selling her own firm, and working with countless other firms to accelerate their success. She gets you to understand what advisory services really are and how they can be woven into a blend of services that deliver great insight and value. Then, she invites you to consider that they may not be right for you.

And that's the key thing: they may not be right for you or your clients.

You are running a business too, and that business has to give you everything you want. Just because you can do something, doesn't mean you should do something.

This book gets you to stop and look at advisory services in a very different way, and it forces you to ask those important questions: What is it? Is it right for me? Is it right for my clients? Is it right for right now? And if it is, what's the best way to move forwards with this?

This is not a book for people who want to jump on the advisory bandwagon. This is about stopping the bandwagon, charting a course that's right for you and creating the best vehicle to get you closer to whatever success looks like for you.

And I sincerely wish you and your clients every success.

James Ashford

Founder of GoProposal and author of *Selling to Serve*

Introduction

How many other accountants are sick of hearing, *"Compliance is dead,"* and we should all move into advisory?

But what if compliance is all you know and all that really interests you? Well, this book will give you an idea of whether you want to make the move into advisory or not. There are few compliance-only accountants, and most offer some sort of advice in addition to simply churning out accounts. This book may help you to do that better, even if you don't want to take it any further. Whilst I believe that the future of accountancy lies in helping clients to change their numbers rather than just recording them, compliance isn't dead yet.

For those who want to introduce advisory services to their clients, then Part 1 of this book provides a simple how-to guide for those wishing to get started. It's based on what I did when building Hudson Business Accountants and Advisers, as well as things I've learned since in my work coaching and mentoring accountants and other business owners. Following the suggestions in this book isn't the only way to do this, but it's one method that has worked for us out in the real world with real business clients. Depending on your definition of advisory services (see Chapter 1), Hudson Business Accountants and Advisers' work was up to 60% advisory work. Use this book as a starting point whilst you find your own way and learn to deliver advisory services in your own style.

If you don't know where to begin with offering advice, then Part 2 is all about what to speak to your clients about. There are also lots of other resources in the Appendices at the end of this book, so you're not on your own.

I've gone out on a limb to include details on software that will help you with some of this journey. Of course, software is constantly being updated and new features added (some such new features have been added whilst I've been writing this book), so do take the time to investigate this area for yourself, perhaps with the help of one of the app-advisory companies mentioned in Chapter 18, as many of my suggestions will be out of date by the time this book is published. However, software is only a tool to help measure the impact of your advice. Most advice will come through your own learning beyond this book, and I've mentioned a few resources throughout and pulled together a list in the Appendices.

Disclaimer regarding software: I'm only one person running two businesses, so I have limited time to test software that I don't use in my own UK-based Minerva Accountants. No supplier has paid to be included in this book, although they may have paid me to write content or present webinars for them in the past, which obviously means that I like their offering (I only work with people I like) and that I'm more familiar with it. I've only included the software I'm most familiar with and that fits with the ethos of the advice in this book. If you know of some helpful software that hasn't been included, then please do drop me an email at hello@hudsonbusiness.co.uk containing a brief paragraph about it and a link to it, so that I can consider including it in my coaching and talks.

As a quick overview to introduce my businesses more fully, I sold Hudson Business Accountants and Advisers in 2017, and I wrote about how we achieved our success in my first book, *The Numbers Business: How to grow a successful cloud accountancy practice.*

I currently own and run Hudson Business Advice as a coaching and consultancy business, helping accountants and bookkeepers to run their own businesses better, and in May 2020, I rose to the pandemic challenge and set up Minerva Accountants in order to support small businesses and their owners that were being told to 'pivot' their business (which we interpreted to mean making large-scale changes to the direction of the business) during lockdown.

As trusted advisers, we have an opportunity to make a real difference to our clients' lives and to help them realise their dreams. How can we deny them our help?

PART 1

HOW TO PROVIDE ADVISORY SERVICES

Part 1 of this book provides a simple how-to guide for those wanting to get started on delivering advisory services, whether to enhance your compliance offering or as an additional source of revenue. It's based on what I did when building Hudson Business Accountants and Advisers, as well as on things I've learned since in my work coaching and mentoring accountants and other business owners.

It's important that you develop your own systems and style, but these are some ideas you may use until you find your own way. I'd also love to hear about other things that have worked for you.

1.
What advisory is & why it's beneficial

A few years ago, we were updating the website for Hudson Business Accountants and Advisers, and I took on a new marketing assistant to help with the task. Part of her job was to do a competitor review. I didn't believe that we had any local competitors offering both a complete accounts package *and* a true business advisory service – the whole package from basic bookkeeping to boardroom – but it turned out that a lot of accountants were marketing themselves as 'business advisers' on the basis that they offered tax advice or advice on obtaining finance. Whilst these are important parts of business advice, they aren't the whole story.

Business advice is much broader than many people think it is

Some types of advice I consider to be an important part of business advice are as follows:

- Systems*
- Technology
- Pricing*
- People
- Legal
- Marketing

- Sales
- Tax
- Finance
- Investment

As you can tell from this diverse list, no small or medium-sized firm can cover everything in-house. I'm not even sure whether a large firm would have sufficient breadth of expertise to cover all of these. Only those asterisked items in the list (systems and pricing) are areas where I consider myself to have in-depth knowledge in both practice and theory.

It may surprise you that I don't list tax and finance as my specialisms, but like most accountants, I'm a generalist who can cover all these areas to an extent and will call in specialists when required. It's important that we know both of the following things:

1. our own limits in each area; and
2. a network of experts whom we can refer to when we reach those limits.

In each chapter, I've included my go-to experts, but you should build your own contact list too.

We're able to offer a holistic service, with the addition of a few specialists to cover areas that we can't offer for legal reasons or because we don't know enough to take on that area beyond an introductory level.

Business advice goes much further than many people think it does

Management accounts still only look at historical data, and forecasting software, whilst useful, can only show different scenarios based on historical numbers. As the Covid-19 pandemic (which is still ongoing at time of writing) has shown us, historical performance is no indication of future success. Businesses have needed to make changes in order to survive. Knowing which changes to make is the key to giving business advice.

Business advisory tools – and there are many mentioned throughout this book (see Appendix 1 for website links for those mentioned) – don't deliver business advice any more than bookkeeping software does accounts, or a hammer and nails constitutes carpentry. They provide invaluable assistance and enable us to serve more clients, because the basics are done for us, but at this point in the development of affordable artificial intelligence (AI), they still aren't up to the standards of an experienced business adviser.

Business advice goes beyond measuring the numbers and progresses to changing those numbers in the real world. Hence the title of this book is *Changing the Numbers*, not *measuring* or *forecasting* them. The title also includes this verb because business advice is useless without action.

Experience is helpful but not essential

Just as a proofreader spots errors that an author misses, we're able to cast an objective eye over a business from the outside. My kids have lived with me doing this all their lives, so as teenagers (at the time of writing), they can even do some of the 'what' determination themselves, noticing how businesses they encounter (mainly shops, restaurants and, of course, their school) could do things more efficiently, and therefore more profitably. They're natural business advisers, but they need more skills and more real-world experience in identifying and suggesting solutions/improvements. They must also develop their communication skills so they're able to explain to the client the benefits of a particular solution. This book will help you with all that, but it shouldn't be your only resource.

You can start by implementing some common ideas into your own business. Although I'm a business coach myself, I still use a business coach too. As she isn't part of my business, she's able to view my work more objectively, in a way that I never will. I'm too wrapped up in the day-to-day work, and she drags me out of the engine room to see the view from the bridge. I always have plenty of ideas to improve my business, and my coach helps me to prioritise them in terms of impact, rather than simply being the latest shiny idea that I've just picked up. If you're a magpie for collecting good ideas, then you'll know exactly what I mean!

As an adviser, you're in a position to make suggestions, but you can't – and shouldn't – force your clients to take a particular course of action in what is, after all, *their* business. Although, if your client never follows your advice, it would suggest you aren't the right adviser for them.

Broaden your thinking

Read broadly around the subject, and if you don't already, start looking at the world differently. See Appendix 2 for some of my favourite books.

It may sound cynical to say, "There is nothing new under the sun," but the same management theories come around again and again in different packaging (demonstrated by the fact that even that quote comes from Ecclesiastes 1:9 in the Bible). Reading more widely will help you to find a format that you can relate to and a system that makes the theory meaningful, so that you can see immediately how to implement it.

As accountants, we have a wealth of clients in different industries. Even if you operate within a niche, you can still see how your individual clients do things very differently. Something that works in one business may well transfer into another industry. Become curious about your clients' businesses beyond the numbers, and it'll soon become evident that certain things almost always lead to success and other things may be worth trying.

When I built my first accountancy practice, I didn't copy other accountancy practices. Instead, I looked outside the profession to see how other businesses operated. I had the benefit of working in other industries for 20 years, as well as seeing the operations of all the clients I had worked with in practice. Whilst I never claimed we weren't like other accountants, it was something our clients often said when referring us, and this is probably the reason for it.

What advice you should give

The advice you give will depend on a number of factors.

First, you need to understand why your client set up or bought their business. There are three main reasons for this:

1. Work-life balance
2. Profit/income
3. Value on sale / retirement

You can only understand this by getting to know your client. If your client has a number of different directors and/or shareholders, they may each have their own motivations.

> I once ran a strategic-planning day for a company with four director-shareholders, only to discover that they had three different objectives between them! It explained why they had all been pulling against each other, to the extent that the business was going nowhere and was seriously underperforming. Once everything was out in the open, we were able to come up with a plan that incorporated two and a half of the objectives.

You also need to distinguish between vanity metrics and real needs. Whilst working with accountants, I often find this to be the case, particularly when sole practitioners tell me they want to build a million-pound practice, but a little more digging unearths that what they actually want is financial security and a decent work-life balance. The million-pound target is an arbitrary figure, which when reached would make them feel successful, but it wasn't their primary motivator.

> Similarly, when doing an annual appraisal with an employee, we were discussing the trappings of success. For him, it was a particular make and model of car. A little more questioning elicited that it didn't have to be a new car and second-hand would be acceptable. A few days later, he turned up at work in his new (to him) car, and with a resulting huge boost in his confidence.

The reason my advice usually starts with systems is that improving efficiency gains time, profit and value, so it hits all three of the primary reasons. Further advice is much more nuanced, but you'll come up with some good ideas that help most of the businesses you work with.

Communicating your advice

Having great ideas on how to improve your client's business isn't enough if you aren't able to communicate them in a way that your client understands.

Accountants are notoriously poor communicators, and we have a lot of our own jargon. Although Minerva Accountants has a Finance for Business Owners course, it's really up to us to learn to speak the language of the business owner. We should listen to the language they use and try to use those phrases too. For example, if they talk about 'buckets' of money when preparing budgets, then you can adapt your vocabulary to ensure that they have a 'bucket' for each type of cost they need to include in their plan.

We have no problem understanding numbers, but so many people are so terrified of numbers that they switch off. We need to find the story behind the numbers, and then talk about it as a narrative in words or even pictures. This is where software can come in, as it can be used to generate graphs for clients who relate more to visual ideas than numerical ones. We still need to find the words to go with the numbers and graphs, and this is why the best advisers are also storytellers.

Why move into advisory?

There are very few compliance-only firms that prepare accounts and tax returns, but do nothing else. Most firms offer some form of advice, even if they don't charge for it. At the other end of the spectrum are numerate business advisers and coaches, who leave it to others to measure the numbers whilst they focus on changing those numbers; this is my main business. I work alongside excellent accountants who want to help their clients but have no desire to move into the advisory arena themselves.

Most accountancy firms sit somewhere along a compliance-advisory spectrum. Depending on what definition of 'advisory' you use, then Hudson Business Accountants and Advisers' business was 60% advisory, but that included management accounts and tax planning.

The reason so many firms already offer an element of advisory is because *every* business wants and needs it. The real-world problem is that not every business can afford it, so we need to decide what services we'll offer to which clients in order to maximise our income.

However, for me, advisory work is about helping business owners to achieve the dreams they had when they first set up their business. When they're a few years in and call on me because they're still working 80-hour weeks, testimonials such as "My wife noticed that I've started singing again" sum up my 'why' in a way that money alone can't.

The keys to being a good business adviser are as follows:

» Be curious – see Appendix 2 for reading ideas, but also look around in the real world

» Be open-minded

» Communicate well

Summary

¤ Advisory is much broader than people think.

¤ Advisory isn't all or nothing; many firms already deliver advisory services, but they don't charge for them.

¤ Solid communication skills are key to good advisory services.

¤ Advisory services aren't for everyone, so think carefully whether they are right for you and your business.

2.
What you need first

Before embarking on your advisory journey, you need solid compliance and suitable clients.

You need to be able to measure the numbers you intend to change, and you need them in a timely fashion so you can see the impact of your actions immediately.

Depending on the client, you (or they) can complete their bookkeeping at least weekly. In some cases, it may be easier to change your bookkeeping processes to handle tasks daily, but until you have at least monthly records, you won't be able to demonstrate the success of your advice.

Data entry

Purchases

Data entry can be speeded up through optical character recognition using software such as Dext Prepare (the software formerly known as Receipt Bank) or Hubdoc. Both work in a similar fashion, and invoices can be uploaded via these methods:

> » Use a fetch facility to download PDFs (portable document format) of invoices in supplier accounts, such as telephone and utility bills. This saves a large amount of time and

hassle through no longer needing to log in to each supplier account in turn to download a PDF of the most recent invoice. As more suppliers use this facility, it'll become more useful. Unfortunately, Hubdoc has just announced that it'll no longer be supporting its fetch feature.

» Forward emailed invoices to a dedicated email address. Once you have everything set up, contact all the suppliers that currently send paper invoices and ask if they can email PDFs in future. This will save paper, so it also has small environmental and cost benefits as well as the efficiency one.

» Scan invoices and upload them into the app. Invoices can be uploaded individually or in bulk.

» Download the appropriate app to your phone, take photographs of all receipts and bills, and then upload the photographs to the app. We have kept an old phone in the office just for this, as it's a much easier way to deal with the fiddly till receipts than trying to unfold them and feed them through a scanner. It's also handy if you have clients who insist on stapling everything!

Supplier rules can be set so that bills are posted consistently to the same account. Value-added tax (VAT) rules can also be set, but it's much more reliable to take the VAT from the individual invoices to ensure compliance with VAT regulations.

Paperless billing is also beginning, through Flux. Suppliers signing up to work with certain banks will automatically have a detailed VAT receipt added to the bank transaction in lieu of a paper till receipt. Another environmental saving.

It's possible for one person to upload the paperwork and for another to code the documents. At Minerva Accountants, we run a paperless operation, so we rely on the client to upload all the paperwork themselves.

Time saving

I've seen many bookkeepers claim to be able to enter bills faster than one of these apps, and in terms of elapsed time, this may well be true, but it's highly unlikely that anybody is going to sit twiddling their thumbs whilst the software processes the documents. This is why we switched our bookkeeping procedures to follow a sequence based on the type of activity, rather than processing one client at a time.

Documents can be uploaded at the press of a single camera button or the forwarding button on an email, which is infinitely faster than typing in every single character by hand. It also eliminates human errors. The combination of the faster entry and fewer errors will save more time than using even the fastest bookkeeper.

Document management (aka filing)

Every invoice needs to be filed for tax and management purposes, but few are ever retrieved. This means that the biggest time saving is made by focusing on faster filing rather than faster retrieval. Electronic copies are perfectly acceptable for Her Majesty's Revenue and Customs (HMRC), so any paper can be shredded by you or the client.

For those who insist on keeping paper invoices, the fastest way to file them is using a box file per week/month/year (depending on the number of transactions). Adding invoices in the order that they're processed means that the oldest will naturally be on the bottom and the newest on top. The bookkeeping system can be used as an index for retrieving paper for any particular supplier.

Sales

Sales invoices can be generated through core bookkeeping software, application programming interfaces (APIs), electronic till software or web shops. With bookkeeping apps being able to raise invoices from the user's phone, there are few reasons these can't be entered into the bookkeeping software in real time.

Cloud software

Modern software such as Xero and QuickBooks Online (QBO) are cloud based, which means they can be accessed simultaneously by the bookkeeper, accountant and business owners. As a result, the data entry can be allocated to those most capable of handling any particular part of it, whether this is the client or the bookkeeper.

Both these bookkeeping apps have APIs to hundreds of business apps that will help to speed up the bookkeeping process and/or provide useful management information.

> At both Hudson Accountants and Advisers and Minerva Accountants, we were and are Xero specialists, so we only need to learn one type of software inside out. Supporting more than one or two types of software will reduce your efficiency, so choose those that are most suitable for your existing clients. If clients prefer to use other software or if Xero doesn't suit their needs for some reason, we can refer them to another accountant who uses more suitable software for their needs. For this reason, I keep half an eye on what's going on with QBO, FreeAgent and Sage.

Bank feeds

Open banking means that most modern banks will have a direct bank feed into Xero or QBO. This effectively uploads the bank statement into the software. Statements can also be uploaded manually in a number of other formats, with comma-separated values (CSV) being the most common.

Sometimes, there can be a glitch in the bank feeds. Some banks provide a running balance as part of their feed, so it's easy to see when this has happened. We also ask clients to confirm their online bank balance at the end of each month. If this doesn't agree with the statement balance on the bookkeeping software, then we may ask for a statement to check the individual transactions. You'll soon learn which banks are more prone to problems.

The beauty of bank feeds is that they'll suggest a match to invoices or follow a rule for such things as salary payments. By the third month, when all supplier rules are set up, we have estimated that using bank feeds saves about 75% of the time taken on posting transactions and reconciling the bank account manually. This means either you can operate more profitably by taking on four times as many clients or you can free up time to offer advisory services.

As a security measure, bank feeds need to be reconnected by the client every 90 days. This means there's a delay whilst we wait for the client to log in to their account to update the feed. The Radar module of FreeAgent reminds the client or accountant to do this before the 90 days is up, but Xero and QBO don't yet. Some banks, such as Starling, provide the client with the reminder to reconnect. I keep meaning to set up some sort of reminder system on my practice's management software. Perhaps I'll have got around to it by the time this book is published!

Suggested bookkeeping routines

The following are my suggestions for helpful daily and monthly bookkeeping routines.

Daily bookkeeping routine

Each activity is carried out for all clients before moving on to the next activity:

» Open post, and sort and scan bills, etc. for each client in turn.

» Code, check and upload all bills, one client at a time.

» Check that the sales interfaces are operating correctly.

» Check that the bank feeds are operating correctly and do reconciliation.

» Check that the other finance feeds are operating correctly and post transactions.

Monthly bookkeeping routine

This is usually done for each client in turn:

» Confirm the online bank balance with the client.

» Do fixed-asset additions/disposals and depreciation.

» Post payroll if this isn't already integrated with the bookkeeping software.

» Post repeating journals automatically.

» Run a Dext Precision (the software formerly known as Xavier) report to check for bookkeeping anomalies.

» Check aged debtors for old or credit balances to be queried, chased or written off.

» Check aged creditors for old or debit balances to be queried, paid or written off.

» If providing full management accounts, then run all non-automated journals and reconcile all balance sheet accounts.

>> Run management accounts (simple or full) in bookkeeping or other software.

>> Run additional reports from other business software packages.

Training

Both Xero and QBO provide *free* training and certification for accountants and bookkeepers, so do take advantage of this. The better you can use the software, the more efficient you'll be and the better you can advise your clients on their own bookkeeping. We also encourage clients' bookkeepers to become certified too.

We provide in-house Xero and Hubdoc training free of charge for our own clients to ensure they do their bookkeeping in the way we like. We do this through a series of videos recorded on Loom that cover the main functions. These are sent out as links on a Word document. For anything else, we send a link to one of the app's own videos or record other Loom videos for our library.

Setting up new clients

We always prefer to set up Xero for our clients ourselves.

We use Move My Books to perform an efficient transfer of up to two years' data from the client's previous software. Even back in the days when we had to pay the whole £200+ fee, this was well worth the time it saved. It's highly unlikely that clients will need to refer back any further, but they can pay to transfer additional years or look at an archived copy on their old software. If they're moving from other cloud software, they can usually keep read-only access for a while or the company will store the data for six years in case of an enquiry from HMRC or other queries.

When setting up from scratch, you can upload a bespoke chart of accounts, but we prefer to use the standard chart of accounts with a list of changes to make for limited companies or sole traders/partnerships.

We set up Hubdoc in-house too.

If a client requires any other apps, then depending on the complexity, we'll set these up or call in a specialist app integrator.

For the first month of using the software, we encourage clients (or their bookkeepers) to contact us for all queries whilst they learn both the software and how we like the bookkeeping to be done. After this, the number of queries reduces, and we continue to handle the bookkeeping queries ourselves, but we refer any software issues directly to Xero (which also owns Hubdoc) unless it's a quick question.

Dext Precision (formerly Xavier)

When I started writing this, Xavier was a relatively new app that I was fortunate enough to see early in its development, as they're based in Bristol, which isn't just a wonderful city but is also the home of a great deal of fintech. Xavier has since been acquired by Receipt Bank and rebranded as Dext Precision. The software connects to Xero and QBO, and it sense checks the bookkeeping in order to allocate a score out of 100. It checks such things as supplier and customer transactions posted to a code other than their usual, and any changes in spending patterns. Syft Analytics also provides some of this functionality.

We use the software in three different ways:

1. We use it to check our own bookkeeping.
2. We use it to check each new client's bookkeeping to see if it's up to the standard we require. This means that we

can either reject it and ask the client to update/tidy it or we can quote to tidy it up for them. No more coping with poor bookkeeping or tidying up free of charge.

3. More recently, we've started to run the software on a monthly basis for clients who do their own bookkeeping, and then giving them their monthly score. This makes us look proactive, provides a monthly excuse for client contact (which increases loyalty), encourages clients to keep their bookkeeping up to date and allows us to spot any bookkeeping weaknesses early on. If bookkeeping does need to be brought in-house, it's easier to do this based on the objective score provided by Dext Precision and the timescale of monthly bookkeeping.

The software isn't foolproof, so we still have to run additional checks, but it saves an awful lot of time, especially when used regularly.

Whilst Dext Precision isn't advisory software in itself, it's essential for us to ensure the quality of the underlying data on which we base our advice.

Other management information

Accounts are often a late indicator (sometimes called a 'lag indicator') in terms of business advice. If a business does the right things, then it will generate profit; the monthly management accounts simply confirm this.

Early indicators (sometimes called 'lead indicators') are more useful. Depending on the area on which advice is being given these can be one of the following:

1. Monitoring your marketing advice, which might involve key performance indicators (KPIs) such as these:

- Flyers distributed or mailshots sent out.
- Speaking events promoting the business or its expertise.
- Social media responses.
- Social media followers.
- Rise score from rise.global. This gives an indication of your social media reach, and the extent that people are interacting with you and the content that you're posting. Take this figure with a pinch of salt; it's easy to increase your score by posting pictures of cute puppies, but this may not convert into enquiries.
- Number of enquiries and their source.
- Number of networking events attended.
- Footfall. That is, how many visitors come to your premises.
- Blogs and articles. Producing these is another way of demonstrating your expertise, and this may be a better format for many prospects or just a different format.

2. Monitoring your sales advice might involve KPIs such as these:

   - Appointments. If you sell sheds, you might find that the appointments booked in your diary for people to see the sheds is a simple measure. You can just look at your diary and say, "Yep, it's full. That's good." You don't even need to count. The diary is full. The page is full. If it's a bit patchy, then it's not so good. KPIs don't need to be 100% accurate to be useful, so look for things that are easy to measure.
   - The number of clients you have, the number of customers on your database, or the number of

transactions per day/week/month. It's useful to track this, as much of your admin cost is per customer, no matter whether they're large or small.

- Turnover/sales.
- Average fee or order value. The higher this is, the better, as this reflects the increased quality of clients and cross-selling.
- Volumes of different products sold.
- Order size. Your average order size might be quite important. Because if it takes you X amount of time and effort to get a sale, you want that sale to be as big as possible. It might be something you want to practise – not selling to more people, but selling more to each of your customers. It's the classic McDonald's, "Would you like fries with that?" When somebody comes in and orders a burger, the staff have a script for trying to sell something extra at the same time, because they've already got the customer through the door.

3. Monitoring your efficiency/productivity advice might involve KPIs such as these:

- Number of jobs/orders outstanding.
- Production time.
- Response time. This is useful for those repairing items or supporting IT systems.
- Time spent on different products or clients.
- Chargeable hours.
- On-time deliveries.
- Rework. That is, how many items need to be redone. This is a useful quality measure.

4. Monitoring your cash-flow advice might involve KPIs such as these:

- Work in progress (WIP) / debtors (also known as lock-up). Your cash is tied up in uninvoiced work and unpaid bills.
- Profit and cash in bank. However, these figures are the result of getting the other indicators right.
- Number of clients on direct debit.
- Profitability of different products. Construction companies might have sales of labour and sales of parts that they want to separate out. They almost certainly want to record the hours they've spent on each job.
- Debtor days. This is a measure of the average time it takes to get paid.
- Cash run-off. This is how long your current cash balance would last without any further income.
- Quick ratio and acid ratio. These are calculations based on the current assets (stock, debtors and cash) available to settle current liabilities (debts).

5. Monitoring your impact on the world, which may be done in terms of the following:

- Carbon footprint.
- Staff happiness.
- Net promoter score. This is a measure of how likely customers are to recommend you.

As you can see, there are all sorts of non-financial indicators, and in addition to the ones listed here, depending on the business, there could be plenty of others that are useful. Look for indicators that are easy to measure. It's more important to monitor trends than accuracy. Is the figure going up or down? And is that the direction it should it be going in?

Advisory clients

Time and again, we hear from those promoting the move to advisory, particularly those selling software, that it will help with this move. Software providers have a clear interest in promoting their products to help make this move, but whilst it can be helpful, advisory is about much more than the software you choose.

Every client needs business advice

The problem is that not every client can afford to pay for the advice that they need.

So, how can you make it more affordable to more businesses?

» Increase your prices generally and provide free advice in the form of helpsheets and webinars. This is what we do at Minerva Accountants. A slight increase in price also moves us away from the tyre kickers who shop around on price rather than value. Sadly, it takes very little to stand out as being 'not like other accountants', so providing a little free support is a good marketing tool. You can afford to throw in a free book such as *Growing by Numbers* by Della Hudson, *The E-Myth Revisited* by Michael Gerber or *Watertight Marketing* by Bryony Thomas.

» Offer group programmes so that clients can share the cost between them. We do this for our courses for accountants (The Numbers Business Online and The ScaleUp Blueprint) and for business owners (Growing by Numbers Online). These are like the webinars, but they also include group coaching and accountability. There

are packages that you can buy, which are detailed in
Chapter 9.

» Automate more of the common advisory work using
software and scripts, so that it can be carried out by
experienced accountants rather than specialist business
advisers (see Chapter 4).

At the moment, advisory work isn't cheap to deliver at scale, but it
adds tremendous value. If we could guarantee value, it would be
much easier to sell (see Chapter 10).

Summary

- ¤ You need a solid compliance foundation before
  embarking on advisory work.
- ¤ Perform weekly or monthly bookkeeping.
- ¤ Automate as much of your data entry as possible to save
  time and money.
- ¤ Consider monitoring non-financial KPIs.
- ¤ Consider free and group programmes to reach more
  people, and also charge more for individual advice.

3.
Pre-advisory – producing the numbers

Now you've got all the numbers up to date, you need to be able to present them in a helpful format. You need to show what the important numbers are currently, what they'll probably be with no further action and what they'll be with certain courses of action.

There's all sorts of software that can help you to present this historical and forecast information, and most small businesses have to start with one or two main suppliers for financial reasons but also because you really do need to spend time learning how to use the software to achieve its full potential.

Management accounts

Your bookkeeping software will have some useful reports of historical information, and this can be compared to a budget/plan in the form of management accounts. Start by producing your own management accounts and learning how to use the report generator to make these more useful. Do you just want figures for the company, or do you want to break them down into departments or in some other way to produce separate figures for different parts of the company?

Pre-advisory

I'm going to be contentious here and declare that telling people their numbers is *not* advisory. Presenting them with numbers in pretty formats is great for their understanding, but the numbers alone aren't advisory. Advisory is about changing those numbers and, most importantly, about *how* to change the numbers. Measuring numbers before and after giving advice is accountancy. Forecasting the change in numbers as a result of our advice is still mainly accountancy as it's putting the story into numbers.

That means management accounts and even preparing forecasts reflecting actions that clients suggest is *not* the same as giving them advice. We need to move away from measuring the numbers and focus on the actions that will change those numbers. We need to change the business story.

For this reason, most of the software that's labelled as 'advisory' software is, in my opinion, still just a tool. A very useful tool, but most of it is about measuring rather than acting. It's still an essential part of your advisory package, but on its own, it isn't advisory.

Spreadsheets

I had an early flirtation with spreadsheets in the form of Lotus 123 and Visicalc, and then I fell head over heels in love when Excel released version 5 with all sorts of user-friendly functionality and macros that could be recorded rather than coded. But these are the tools of my youth, and whilst there will always be a place in my heart for spreadsheets, I now prefer something a little more sophisticated for most regular tasks.

Spreadsheets definitely have their uses for one-off operations, but if we're going to take advisory work seriously, then we need up-to-date numbers and calculations at our fingertips. Updating numbers in spreadsheets and tweaking formulae every month or more frequently isn't cost-effective when the right software can do this for you instantly.

Software

This section details the software I've found useful. It isn't the only software, by any means, and of course, software keeps being updated. This is software that I like and that suits the way I prefer to work, so please do your research above and beyond this.

As always, start by using the software on your own business, as these are the numbers that you're most familiar with, so you'll get a good feel for how the software makes predictions, how realistic it is and therefore how useful it is likely to be. Any machine learning will be based on historical information, which – whilst a good start – isn't always a good assumption in a growing or changing company. It's certainly not reliable when trying to forecast for a business during an unprecedented pandemic, but it's often a good start.

I haven't included prices, but it's a big selling point for me if there's a low-cost entry into offering advisory services through only needing to buy one licence at a time. Bulk licences are all very well, but you don't want to pay for 10, or even five, whilst you're still figuring out how to deliver advisory services your way.

Including training is also helpful as it ensures you can make the most of the software, whether that's solely using it yourself or helping your clients to use it too (depending on the software in question, as some packages are for use by the adviser only and others allow the work to be split between adviser and client). As a result, this increases your chances of making a success of your new advisory services.

Xero

Xero is predominantly for historical data and conventional management reporting. It has a budgeting capability and tracking codes that can be used for measuring departmental or regional performance.

Once you've agreed a profit-and-loss budget, it can be uploaded into Xero and compared against the actual results for the company and also by department.

Xero can produce a basic management accounts pack with a selection of financial KPIs in the form of its Business Snapshot and Business Performance reports. If you give the right advice, you'll change the numbers on these reports.

During the Covid-19 pandemic (which is still ongoing at the time of writing), Xero accelerated the release of its cash-flow forecast. This is good for forecasting 7–30-day cash balances when cash is particularly tight. It uses the due dates on sales invoices and purchases, but it doesn't include VAT, salaries or other taxes. If an invoice is overdue, you need to put in an expected date.

All this is included within core Xero, and much more is available through connecting to some of the other apps in this chapter. Licences can be purchased one at a time, and training/certification is online, along with 24/7 support.

QuickBooks Online (QBO)

Like Xero, QBO is primarily for historical data. It also allows you to upload budgets, but it doesn't have the same tracking facility.

QBO can produce a basic management accounts pack, and some visual users prefer the on-screen presentation.

However, QBO has no forecasting capability, as this is reserved for the desktop version.

Like Xero, there's much more functionality available through connecting to some of the other apps in this chapter. Licences are available one at a time, and training/certification is also included for accountants.

Sage

It would be hard to ignore such a popular piece of software, but without its own forecasting functionality, Sage is best linked to some of the other forecasting software. There are different versions of each Sage software product, so you need a clear understanding of whether your particular app and version will link into the software.

FreeAgent

FreeAgent is excellent for the small services- or subcontractor-type client, and it produces some useful figures, such as tax estimates. Whilst FreeAgent doesn't generally have as many bells and whistles as Xero and QBO, it does have a rather smart feature called Radar.

Radar cash flow is useful for forecasting up to 90 days ahead, and it's based on the due dates of invoices and bills, recurring bills, tax calcs, salaries, etc. It also has some useful alerts, such as notifying the user when the company is likely to run out of cash.

Although this only forecasts 90 days ahead, it's all done automatically, so it's very useful for helping clients to stay on top of a few key numbers.

FreeAgent also has some wonderful helpsheets, articles and infographics you can share with your clients.

Fluidly

Fluidly syncs information from both Xero and QBO. It handles forecasting for up to 12 months, but I like it best for 90-day cash-flow forecasting.

Fluidly utilises some clever algorithms to base forecasts of future invoicing and payment performance on historical figures.

Machine learning means that the algorithms, and therefore the predictions, are likely to become more accurate with time. The software produces a more comprehensive forecast than other apps, but it did produce some odd numbers when I first connected my own accounts. I'd like to have a better understanding of the algorithms before relying on them for automatic cash forecasting, but as I've said previously, these automatic forecasts should be viewed as a starting point. Fluidly is great for scenario planning, where you can play with the financial impact and timing of things such as recruiting a new sales person or taking on premises.

Float

Float is a short-term-cash-flow app. It can easily be connected to Xero, QBO or FreeAgent through an API. The short-term cash flow is based on the due dates of sales invoices and purchases, but it has the facility to calculate a longer-term forecast based on user input. Overdue invoices need to be allocated an expected due date to be included in the forecast properly.

Float only forecasts cash flow, so all data input manually needs to include the VAT figures and be entered into the period of receipt, not that of invoicing. For instance, if you're forecasting sales of £5,000 for January that are payable in 30 days, then you'll need to enter £6,000 into February. Regular users will become comfortable with this. As Float doesn't handle VAT rates, it also doesn't forecast the amount of VAT that needs to be paid. This is potentially a big cash payment, and yet it still needs to be forecast manually.

Scenario planning is available so that you can demonstrate the impact on cash flow of any actions.

Float pricing allows you to test the waters with a single client before committing to larger numbers for bigger discounts. It also provides free online certification (this took me 40 minutes).

It recommends that the software is maintained mainly by the business owner with the accountant adding insights.

Float provides some emails, web content, etc. to help share the benefits of the service with your clients.

Futrli

Futrli has two levels of functionality: Predict and Adviser. The data is synchronised from Xero, QBO or MYOB, and Sage will soon follow.

Futrli Predict is a three-way forecasting app. This means it offers both a historical and forecast profit and loss, a balance sheet and cash flow. After a little bit of set up, the software is simple to use, and training is now included. It populates predictions automatically across the P&L and balance sheet as part of the set-up, but then you can add your own too.. For each line you add, you can define the VAT rate and normal payment terms.

This is another step up from the cash-flow apps, and it offers full business forecasting for up to three years. Having spent 20 years in industry, I'm more used to five-year forecasting, but three-year forecasting is probably enough for the small-business market. Budgets/forecasts can be uploaded or calculated in a number of ways.

Futrli Advisor allows 10-year forecasting and provides some useful alerts. This is where its scenario forecasting sits.

The nice thing about Futrli is that it offers both dashboards (for on-screen client meetings) and reports, so that clients have something to take away and review.

Futrli also has a helpful peer group called Peer.

Fathom

I first came across Fathom – a beautiful management accounting pack with stunning reports – about five years ago, and it still delights me.

Like Futrli, it synchronises with Xero, QBO and MYOB. It also produces a three-way forecast, and data for forecasts can be imported or calculated in a number of ways. The VAT and payment terms are set up as you enter each line individually.

I've also included this as advisory software in Chapter 4 because the comparisons also generate a simple narrative with some basic advice to help you scale your advisory offering.

As well as having the most beautiful reports, Fathom allows you to purchase just one licence at a time, so there's no financial barrier to getting started with it.

Syft Analytics

A recent entry into the forecasting arena, Syft Analytics has various levels of functionality. The free version offers some pretty reports, but forecasting functionality is only included at the first paid level. The subscriptions are for unlimited clients and users, which is great value once you have enough on board, but there's no cheap way to start off with just one or two clients.

Senta

I've included Senta here in the pre-advisory section, as although it's predominantly about practice management, it has some useful features.

Senta can be set up to integrate with Xero at a client level, which means it has a useful dashboard of KPIs. This can be used in two ways:

1. To give a quick view of the KPIs for each business where full advisory software isn't already being used. This can be used for starting conversations.

2. To set alerts for advisory clients (e.g. where cash is a problem, you can set an alert if it goes below a certain amount or if debtor days go above a certain value).

This is included in the basic Senta fee, and it's a useful add-on for those just getting into advisory.

I'd love to conclude that a particular app is the app for tracking and forecasting numbers for advisory, but even without the rapid rate of change in technology, there's no clear winner.

Summary

You probably can't afford to invest in all of these apps, especially initially, so here's what I suggest you do:

- ¤ Try them all and maybe others besides.
- ¤ Use any free training available to help you to get the most out of the product.
- ¤ Speak to your software account managers and assess how much they'll support you and the business you want to build. Do they really understand accountants and advisory, or are they just selling software?
- ¤ Start having conversations with your clients (see Chapter 16) during your trial period, to find out exactly what they need, and choose your first piece of software accordingly.
- ¤ Treat your software as a part of a toolbox. As you move into a new home, you gradually start to buy tools. Maybe you get a couple of screwdrivers and a single hammer before buying a wider set and a more expensive drill. You refine your choice to get the best tool for the job and for you.

¤   You'll have a favourite tool, but don't rule out others
    where they're more appropriate. I have a favourite knife
    when cooking; it's not particularly better than the other
    knives in my knife block, but the size and weight suit
    me, which means that I do better work with it. However,
    I still use all the knives at different times when they're
    more suitable for different tasks. It's just the same with
    software.

4.
People & software

Skills

The skills required to deliver advisory services may not be the same as those required to prepare historical accounts and tax returns. This means that your best accountants may not necessarily make your best advisers.

Being a good adviser requires curiosity and interest. You'll need to find out not only all about the existing business but also about the area in which you're advising them. Whilst auditing skills may help with this, we aren't required to be independent and are able to take statements more at face value, rather than being constantly suspicious.

A good adviser will have a wealth of expertise to draw on, but they should also be able to think outside the box when looking for solutions. This is sometimes a challenge for accountants, who have often chosen a role that follows fixed procedures in a profession that discourages deviation.

Another ability a good adviser will need is having good listening skills to understand what problem the client is trying to solve. This should be coupled with good questioning skills to dig deeper into the issue to unearth all the relevant information. This information will be essential for both understanding the matter and devising the right solution that will fit the organisation well.

People skills are another necessary element of this role: firstly, when getting information from people, and subsequently, when it comes to implementing any new procedures, software or whatever the solution is. Your client's people will almost certainly need to be involved in the change.

These skills aren't always common in the accounting world, so you may need to look at adding them to your team through training or recruitment. Coaching qualifications can help your team to improve their skills in these areas, and I've certainly found it useful.

Expertise

You will, of course, need to understand the matter on which you're advising.

Expertise can be obtained through first-hand experience or through study of a particular area. Many subjects can be studied second-hand on courses or learned third-hand through books. However, once the initial expertise has been acquired, it's essential to remain up to date with the latest theories and trends.

The general rule is that, to become an expert, it takes 10,000 hours or approximately five years of full-time study. Just think how long it took you to qualify as an accountant, let alone how long it took you to become good at your job.

Experience is a great teacher, but it may only show one way of doing things. Study will include many more possibilities, but it will rarely be in as much depth as having been there and done it. This is why a combination is often the best approach, and it also accounts for why many business advisers are older, as it takes a while to acquire sufficient experience in each area.

Communication

It's no good having brilliant ideas if you can't share these competently with your clients. Most ideas are communicated initially through a verbal presentation and explanation, before being followed up by a written report. It's important to use simple, accessible language that your clients can understand. Now isn't the time to sound clever, or your client may not implement your advice, so there will be no benefits for them, only your costs. The real value of your advice is in what happens after you've presented your report.

As many accountants are introverts, they may not be comfortable with verbal communication. Never fear, I know two communication experts who can help you to present and explain your findings and recommendations. Alexandra Bond Burnett is a bookkeeper with a theatrical background, whilst Scott Johnston is an escaping lawyer (see Appendix 1 for website details). They both run group and individual training to help accountants improve their communication and presentation skills.

Personality profiling

If you're familiar with personality profiling through your recruitment and other human resources (HR) processes, you'll have recognised that the ideal profile for an accountant isn't the same as that of an adviser. As always, start by producing your profile for the new role. If you're trying to use your existing team to cover the new work, then you can compare their current profiles to the ideal one and start a discussion from there.

Personality profiling isn't an exact science and so is best carried out by an expert. We use Joanne Wharam of Smart Support for Business (see Appendix 1 for website details) to help with DiSC (dominance, influence, steadiness and conscientiousness) profiling. This helps us to get the most out of our team.

Beyond your team

It may well be that you don't have the right people in your existing team to move into advisory services. In this case, you can recruit, use an external coach or consultant, or outsource the whole advisory function. There's more about working with experts in Chapter 9.

Software

There's all sorts of software that purports to be advisory software, but most of it is just a tool to help you measure the historical numbers and forecast the results of your advice. I've already reviewed this type of software in Chapter 3. For me, there's limited software available for dealing with the pure advisory aspect, which is about *changing* the numbers.

Clarity and Fathom software both suggest actions that will change the numbers. Clarity links to your historical accounting software and focuses on seven key indicators measuring profit, asset value and productivity. It has simple sliders to show the impact of changing one or more indicators. This enables the adviser to have a conversation, but the software also produces a plan, a report on the agreed actions, and some suggestions or advice on how to go about this. Clarity is more than software, and it also includes training and a community to help with the advice itself.

Fathom started life as reporting software, and then it added forecasting. The reports include a few suggestions on how to change the numbers; for instance, a high debtor-day measurement would prompt an idea on how to improve this.

Other advisory software

There's a lot of pre-advisory software that will measure historical results and key indicators and then flag when certain indicators can be improved.

Satago has a dashboard and reports that help to measure and highlight clients who may benefit from credit control reviews, software or outsourced services. The company of that name also provides training on how to do this.

Capitalise offers a dashboard that helps to measure and highlight clients who may benefit from funding through the Capitalise platform and its panel of lenders.

Senta practice management software includes a dashboard with a number of indicators that might encourage you to offer solutions and advice.

Management accounts and forecasting software that can be used to measure the impact of your advice includes the accounting platforms of Float, Futrli, Fluidly, Syft Analytics and Fathom.

Templates and helpsheets

To help your team, you may wish to set up your own processes, templates and helpsheets. The second half of this book will help you with ideas for the type of advice you may be able to give.

The limitations of software

Software can be great for handling the 80% of advice that comprises basic, recurring business guidance, but it isn't yet suitable for handling everything. It's a good way to start offering advisory services or to scale up. Have a look at the options available and decide how you could use one or more in your business.

Summary

- ¤ The skills required by an accountant and an adviser may not be the same.

- ¤ Personality profiling may help you to assess your existing team.

- ¤ The team members may need training on presentation and communication skills.

- ¤ You may need to look beyond your team.

- ¤ Software can help you to scale up your offering.

- ¤ Software can't replace individual business advice from an expert.

5.
Leading by example

Before embarking on advisory work, it's worth making sure you have your own house in order. Not only will this give you a better, more profitable business but it'll make you a good case study for the services you're trying to sell.

Make your business your first advisory client and work through all the chapters in the second part of this book to ensure that you're a good advertisement for your services and to iron out any teething problems in how you deliver these improvements in practical terms. Having implemented improvements in your own business will also make you more authentic when talking to clients about the pros, cons and how-tos.

Experience the reality of changing a business with a team who don't like change, with limited budgets and, most of all, with limited time. There are too many people talking the talk and not enough of them walking the walk. When I wrote about how I had started and grown my first business in *The Numbers Business*, people soon started approaching me for my coaching and consultancy services because I had proven practical experience and success.

When training your own team to run advisory sessions, as a result of your own implementation, they'll have first-hand experience of many of the outcomes that you want for your clients. Although they may not have run a business themselves, they'll have a better understanding of what good looks like if they're surrounded by it on a daily basis.

This chapter includes some specific advice for running a good accountancy practice, but you should also deploy all the relevant advice from the second half of this book and my other books; I won't repeat that content here.

I'll briefly talk you through our The ScaleUp Blueprint model, which I use on one of our group coaching programmes. For more information, you can, of course, join the programme itself to prepare your business to better help others.

Systems

In order to run a good accountancy practice that's independent of the owner(s), you'll need to replace your brain with some sort of automation and other processes. I talk about mapping processes and then writing procedures, training, delegating and automating in Chapter 6, but there's some particular automation that helps you to run a more efficient and profitable practice.

Practice-management solutions

To run your practice more efficiently, you may need to put systems in place. This may be simple procedures and delegation, or it may require an investment in automation.

Over the last few years, several affordable practice management systems have been made available to help you offer a slick, efficient service to your clients. AccountancyManager, Senta and Pixie are useful for small practices if you don't already have something in place to manage your processes, reminders and deadlines.

Compliance

See Chapter 2 for suggestions on systemising, automating and delegating your compliance work, as well as Chapter 15 on more general efficiencies.

Advisory

See Chapter 4 on advisory software and staffing.

Lead generation

See Chapter 10 on marketing advisory services, and for more general marketing, see Chapter 19 and my first two books (*The Numbers Business* and *Growing by Numbers*).

Engaging clients (onboarding)

You should have a clear process in place from the initial enquiry, and on through the discovery meeting, quotation and the first 100 days. Practice Ignition (app) can help to automate part of this.

You and your team

For your team, see Chapter 4 and my first two books (*The Numbers Business* and *Growing by Numbers*).

Pricing

See Chapter 13 on pricing. Go Proposal is very useful for setting prices and presenting them well.

Summary

¤ Be your own first advisory client:

- Try out the techniques first-hand.
- Be a good role model for your clients.
- Show your team what good looks like.

¤ Work through The ScaleUp Blueprint or a similar model to review all the processes in your own practice.

¤ Use robust practice management and onboarding solutions to take care of the two biggest processes in your own business.

6.
Delivering advisory services

So you've got your first advisory client, but what are you going to do with them?

A typical session

You'll soon discover your own way of working, but here's a typical session for me:

- » Review the results since your last session and measure impact.
- » Listen to your client regarding any changes or new problems.
- » Prioritise the new problems in your list.
- » Consider the options.
- » Run what-if scenarios for larger projects if required. Smaller projects can often be implemented quickly and cheaply, so it isn't worth spending time on forecasting the outcome if it's an obvious improvement.
- » Agree what actions are needed for the next period: either a decision, whole actions or just the first step in a bigger project.
- » Book the time of the next meeting/review.

The full programme

Every client will have different requirements, but I like to have a standard list of things that I look at until their true priorities become clear. It also means I can have a lot of useful material and resources ready behind the scenes.

The idea is definitely *not* to follow this list no matter what's going on in the business. It's just a list to ensure all the key areas are covered over a period of time. You may never reach the end of the list if a few sessions on a key area reap sufficient benefits for the client. As always, there are areas that will have high rewards.

Part 2 of this book looks in detail at the 13 main areas for you (also listed as follows), plus there are others included in my *Growing by Numbers* book, but you may have other things that you want to include or you may prefer to split the topics differently:

1. Clarifying the vision
2. Changing the cash flow
3. Changing the pricing
4. Changing the time – time management, team working, the Pomodoro technique and other useful techniques, time blocking, DiSC profiling (also with key customers), appraisals, and training
5. Changing the efficiency – automation, etc.
6. Changing the funding – capital advisory and becoming proactive
7. Changing the tax – don't put the tax cart before the profit horse, and research and development (R&D)
8. Changing the value – automation, etc.
9. Changing the marketing – strategy, avatar, routine and recycling
10. Changing the sales – sales conversion

11. Changing customer service / quality

12. Changing the overheads – remote working, outsourcing, part-time roles, etc.

13. Changing the rest – pensions, investments, HR, legal, mergers and acquisitions, and succession planning

Prioritising

It isn't possible to do everything at once, so weigh up urgent vs important areas. Consider the potential impact of a project, the time to pay back, the time required, the cash required and what other resources will be necessary.

Generally, the biggest impacts come from bigger projects, but you may come across some quick wins, so it's good to get these in to free up your client's time or generate more cash to implement the larger projects, as well as to provide encouragement.

The things classed as urgent and important should obviously be top of your list to implement. If something is urgent but unimportant, then delegate if possible *and* put something in place so that it won't recur or is easily dealt with.

> *With important areas, big wins may take time, but some small quick wins are good for morale, and let's face it, they help to justify your fee.*

The initial meeting

This is the first paid session, not the free initial meeting that all accountants offer as part of their sales process. You should already have some idea of the main problems as seen from the client's point of view, so you can have some questions ready to explore these areas in more depth.

Part of what you need to establish is whether these are the true problems or whether they're the consequence of other problems. For instance, clients may come to you complaining that they're working 80 hours per week, which seems like a time management problem, but it may be that they don't charge enough, so it's really a pricing problem; perhaps it's because they're unable to delegate, so it's a leadership problem; or there may be a more specific systems problem that's ruining their efficiency.

Have some open questions ready for each of your main advisory areas.

Also, although this is mainly about information gathering, have some advice ready that will give an instant improvement in at least one area. Clients need to be rewarded with some quick wins to keep them motivated to work through the bigger projects, which will take more time to show results but also will make the real difference in the longer term. It's something that also helps to confirm your expertise.

Your tone

Accountants are notoriously poor communicators, and some people get this automatically, whilst others need to work on it.

Yes, we're experts and charge accordingly, but we also have to motivate our clients to get the actions implemented, so they need to know that we're on their team. They've usually come to us with a specific problem, but we mustn't forget that, to them, the rest of their business is probably operating well. Whether it's a poor business or a good one that's operating sub-optimally, the client will still have an emotional attachment to it. Whilst we're acting as a critical friend, we mustn't be seen to criticise the business.

I'm not a violent person, but if you were to criticise one of my children, you'd see my rapid transformation into a tigress, as opposed to being a competent adult who's open to new ideas. The same applies to any criticism of the business that I've built from scratch and, definitely, to certain pet projects within it.

Consider your words carefully. If you think you may have something difficult to say, then perhaps rehearse it beforehand. Talk about facts and not emotions. This is why Xavier (Dext Precision) is one of my favourite tools when discussing the wreck that some people call 'bookkeeping'. Having a Xavier score helps to take the emotion out of any advice, so you and your client can focus on improvements that will change that number. You can find all sorts of ways to evaluate aspects of businesses, or you can make up your own scoring systems in addition to the accounts.

We need to combine hard numbers, skills and facts with soft skills, so as to consider the personal impact. If you've ever had to make anybody redundant, you'll understand the need to do things correctly and legally but also to show a certain amount of genuine sympathy for the individual who is out of a job because their role is redundant. Giving hard advice can sometimes be like this too. On the other hand, business owners are often grateful to us for providing facts and figures to support a difficult decision that they would struggle to take alone because they're too involved in the situation.

Group sessions

Business advice is best given when considering only one company, as you can go into much greater depth, but you may sometimes prefer to do it in group sessions. The main reasons for doing this are because you have limited business advisory resource or to make it affordable to more clients. There are different reasons for and ways to run group advisory sessions.

- **Marketing** – You may wish to hold an open session to demonstrate your expertise. This is why Minerva Accountants run our *Money Matters* webinars.
- **Mastermind** – In a multidisciplinary group, you can benefit from a variety of inputs to any situation and not just rely on your own expertise. The problem with these is controlling the session:

  - Have the right mix so everybody can input and everybody can benefit.
  - Have the right level of expertise in the group so nobody is talking nonsense.
  - Chair the group well so nobody is talking too much.
  - Have clear rules for the group so everything is confidential and nobody feels victimised by suggestions being presented too aggressively.

Whilst 'masterminds' may seem a good way to offer business advice whilst you too are learning, you may wish to get an external facilitator in to ensure that the group offers a safe and productive space for all participants.

- **Set programmes** – These are like the training programmes we run for accountants and business owners. They follow a predetermined course of common subject areas, and so it's harder for them to allow for any particular problems that participants may be experiencing, other than in a shared question-and-answer session. The benefit is that it's a cheaper way to offer business advice for those in the early stages of their business who need to learn everything or for those who just want general advice to tweak their business, even though they don't have any major problems. For the right audience, these can offer much better value than individual business advice.

Online vs offline

When I ran Hudson Business Accountants and Advisers, we offered all our advice sessions and Money Matters sessions face to face. This is because we drew most of our clients from the local area. You can offer business-advice meetings at you premises or the client's. Sometimes, it can be easier to see problems when visiting the client, but it may also be harder for them to hide away from distractions.

Online sessions are much more flexible and save travel time. These days, I offer coaching by telephone or Zoom, because my niche means I work with accountants who are further afield, and some aren't even in the UK. We also run online webinars and group programmes for the same reason. If you too have clients and/or a target market that isn't local, then this may well be a better option.

Even when offering online advice, it can be helpful to have at least one session or even just a cup of coffee in person, if that's practical, so I try to meet up with clients at conferences or as I travel around. It isn't essential to meet up, but it does help to consolidate relationships.

Action plans

I like to take notes during meetings, as I have the memory of a flip-flop. These notes are for my benefit only and are not intended to be shared with the client. Some advisers like to record their Zoom sessions and send a recording to the client when they've finished. I'd be happy to do this for their benefit, but for myself, I prefer the written word.

Around 15 minutes before the meeting, I clear my desk and read up on our last session. This doesn't just refresh my memory but it also helps me to get a feel for the business and the owner again, as well as switching my mindset into adviser mode.

During the session itself, I start a new set of notes by copying in the brought-forward actions, and we discuss each of those and measure the results where appropriate. Any new actions for me or the client are marked with an asterisk.

We then move on to any new issues or the next phase of the old issues, and inevitably, a few more asterisks are added.

As we wind up the meeting, I copy the asterisked items to a list at the bottom of the page, and we agree which actions the client will take before the next meeting. Don't try to add everything to your lists. I like to work with fortnightly meetings, so one to three actions is about right. The rest just sit on the issues list to be discussed and actioned at some undetermined future date.

For a one-off session, such as a strategic-planning day, we'll complete a workbook throughout the day.

Although I may pick up actions for myself – such as sending a particular piece of information, a template or a referral – I don't issue any sort of report. If this were to be required, I'd record the session and pass it to my personal assistant (PA) to prepare a draft report, as it wouldn't be a good use of my time.

Financial plans

Financial reports and forecasts are a different matter. Most people can't hold numbers in their heads, so it's good to combine an action plan or strategic plan with a professional-looking set of numbers.

There's plenty of software designed for this purpose,
so take a look at Chapters 3 and 4, and then choose two
to three to have in your toolbox.

Referrals to other experts

I started off by confessing that I'm a generalist. Whilst I can offer a basic level of advice on most business issues, this may not be enough, and that's where my network comes in. For every aspect of business advice that you want to offer, you should have an expert to whom you can refer clients or whom you can bring in to support you.

Sometimes, it may be that you really can't offer advice at this stage or it may be a specialist area, such as law or financial planning, so you'll introduce your expert right at the beginning.

On other occasions, you can give the advice, but your client will need extra resource to implement it. An obvious area is recommending a new business app that requires a specialist to set it up or to project manage the changeover. It's important that you have a network of experts who can provide the best advice to your clients, rather than struggling through in an area where you aren't an expert.

Summary

¤   Feel free to use my typical session until you develop something that works better for you and your clients.

¤   Familiarise yourself with all the areas in Part 2 of this book.

¤   Prepare well for your meetings.

- ¤ Consider offering group advisory sessions in different formats.
- ¤ Ensure there's a list of actions at the end of each session or nothing will change.
- ¤ Have a network of experts whom you can refer to when necessary.

7.
Selling profitable advisory services

Setting client expectations for advisory services

What you deliver to your clients will depend on the type of services you want to offer. The important thing is to set out your stall and be clear what you will and won't do, as well as what's included in the fee.

At Minerva Accountants, we set expectations by offering three different packages:

1. 'No Frills' is our minimum viable product, and it consists of just year-end compliance and a monthly bookkeeping health check on Xavier. There's no promise of advice, so I'm quite happy that anything I can't answer off the top of my head or with one of our helpsheets is chargeable. I usually give a straightforward answer, so we're not being unhelpful, and I end it by saying, "Get back to me if you still have questions." By making this require a second interaction, it's easier to tell them, "We can do X, and it'll cost £Y."

   Oh, and we do a free monthly webinar series called *Money Matters* and a weekly business tip too.

2. Our standard 'Business Focus' package is still mainly compliance related, although this is focused much more on monthly interactions than annual ones. With a higher fee and up-to-date information, we're able to spot opportunities a little more proactively, but any advice is still mainly reactive.

3. Our 'Virtual FD' (financial director) package is where we can provide individual attention and discover ways to improve the business. This is because we deal mainly with small-business owners who are great at what they do, but who aren't necessarily good at running a business.

Charging a good fee allows us the time (and the purchase of some software) to do the following:

> » Talk to the client and identify any pain points for them (adviser).
> » Measure the cost/extent of that pain (accountant).
> » Explore possible solutions (adviser).
> » Forecast expected outcomes that can be quantified (accountant).
> » Implement changes (possibly at an extra cost) (adviser).
> » Measure the actual outcomes to demonstrate the benefit of the advice (accountant).

As you can see, we flit between adviser and accountant modes, which is why we can offer a service that non-accountants can't. It's the forecasting ability that allows us to define the potential benefits of using our services, but it isn't the service itself.

Winning new work

We're in the privileged position of being able to look behind the scenes at each of our client's businesses through scrutinising the numbers and talking to the client. We have a captive market for business advice, so we just need to decide how to start the conversation.

We can do it manually by calculating debtor days or slow payments, and then open a conversation about what they could do with more cash, especially if they have overdrafts and large interest payments, but also if they want more cash for business or personal plans.

There's also some software available that will connect to your clients' Xero and other software so as to produce and prioritise some of these KPIs automatically. This is the software mentioned in Chapter 4, which provides potential advice as well as identifying the area to discuss.

If you already subscribe to some such software, then you may be able to run a free basic report and send it to your clients.

Navigating difficult conversations

All these things help you to start a conversation:

- "We noticed that..."
- "This means that... Is it something that keeps you awake at night?"
- "What if we were able to improve it by...?"

You can then start to discuss your pricing models.

At the moment, there's only one software package that's purely advisory and can help you to have this conversation. This is Clarity, which provides seven KPI sliders that can be moved and discussed with the client, who can then see the impact of changing certain profit, value and productivity indicators. Once agreed, the Clarity software also allows you to prepare an action plan for your client.

This action plan means you don't need an experienced business adviser for all of your clients, so it can be a good way of getting into the advisory market and also scaling up your advisory work, as it can now be done by an accountant who has been around the block, rather than the most experienced and expensive person in the business.

Communicating new pricing models or structures

> I was recently approached to work with an accountant who had been offered a buyout, but he felt that there was a better way. We discussed how the business could be modernised to give him a better work-life balance *and* to increase the ultimate sale value when he's finally ready to sell. We were then able to take the increased value (based on the rate I got for selling my own business) plus the future profit he would get to keep, and then compare the total with my fee to see whether it was a logical decision. Without that comparison, my fee would have looked like a very high cost.
>
> Whilst my fee was calculated based on time spent, my service was sold based on the value to the client.

There are several models that you can use:

- **Compliance plus** – You can provide content passively in the form of helpful webinars and e-newsletters. You can answer reactively using prewritten helpsheets and simple frequently-asked-question (FAQ) videos. This allows you to help people via a one-to-many model with minimum cost to the adviser, so it can be quite profitable just by wrapping it up in a higher basic fee.

Selling this model relies on having some good case studies on how it has helped other clients.

- **A one-to-many programme** – You can build your own or buy one in from Entrepreneurs' Circle, The Gap or our Growing by Numbers Online (see Appendix 1 for website details). These each come with all the videos and discussion material you need to help each of your clients grow their business and deal with common areas of concern.

  This can be sold under a separate fee to the compliance work.

- **Proactive retainer** – You can explicitly agree on a business-advice package to include certain reports, meetings, etc., but please include a commitment from the client to implement the actions agreed. With our Growing by Numbers Online and other programmes, we insist that the business owner sets aside half a day a week to work on the actions generated throughout the programme. You should do the same.

  This is usually sold for an inclusive fee, depending on the frequency of reporting, meetings and the underlying compliance work. This is a premium product as the advice is offered on a one-to-one basis. This can be the retainer, and if additional support is needed to move a project along faster, it can be charged as extra.

- **Ad hoc** – You can offer support for individual projects. These are the easiest to sell, as there's usually a very clear pain point and a solution, so everybody can agree the value (financial and non-financial) fairly easily.

Client case studies on wins and losses

It's important to generate client case studies for your marketing. They'll also make your website stand out.

Having case studies provides third-party evidence that your advice works, but it also gives examples of how you can help.

One of the first exercises we do is to look at customer/segment/ product profitability. We can easily demonstrate that getting rid of clients worth £X to you will only impact your profit by £Y. This can mean either turning a loss into a profit or freeing up time to make further improvements in the business.

> We worked with one client to get rid of 22% of their clients whilst reducing profit by only 6%. In theory, they could have saved a whole salary, but the idea was to churn unprofitable clients and replace them with more profitable ones. We also advised them to introduce a minimum fee.
>
> The first time they did this, they were very reluctant, and we had to put together scripts to help them. Once they had finished the exercise, they were keen to repeat it in six months' time (I had suggested annually), as they had started to notice how poor the next level of clients were compared to the higher-quality ones they were bringing in. They also increased their minimum fee further.

Another common exercise is pricing. We can show the exercise on paper, and you may have seen one of my pricing talks, but until you actually do it, it's hard to know just how many clients will go and the impact on time and/or profit. Having case studies can encourage clients to follow through on this action. Without exception, every client who has carried out a repricing exercise with me has been eager to repeat it the following year.

Rolling this out across the firm

First, start with your own firm. Everything that you advise your clients can be tried and tested in your own business initially.

Subsequently, roll it out with your best client, and then the next few. That way, you can start to build your checklists/audits, scripts and templates. Once you have these, you can write the full procedure and deploy it out further through other members of your team.

Every member of your team should be familiar with your compliance-plus resources so that they can identify opportunities to help clients. The standard information can be emailed out with a message to clients stating that they should get in touch if they still have further queries. These further queries then become chargeable work.

The simple phrase to remember is this: "Yes, we can help with X, and that will cost £Y / £Y per hour."

Summary

We now have the following:

- ¤ Places to find data to open the conversation.
- ¤ Ideas on scripts to start the conversation.
- ¤ Models to provide advisory work.
- ¤ Conversations about how much that will cost.
- ¤ How to roll out advisory work further so that at least some of it can be done by cheaper people, plus automation to help.

8.
Compliance plus

Not everybody wants to offer full compliance services, but many accountants want to be a little more proactive about helping their clients. Fortunately, advisory isn't an all-or-nothing decision, so you can pick and choose to offer the services that you want to. It's your business, so be clear which services you want to offer and why.

There are all sorts of ways you can help your clients without setting yourself up to operate advisory as a whole income stream. If you offer mainly compliance services but throw in some useful advice as you spot it or as your clients ask, then you'll be able to charge a higher fee because you're clearly delivering better value than your compliance-only competitors.

Resources

As a business owner, you'll have some first-hand experience of running a business.

As a curious accountant working with lots of different types of business, you'll have a lot of second-hand knowledge. You can borrow ideas from one industry to help a client in a completely different sector. When I set up my first practice, I tried to replicate very little that I'd learned in traditional accountancy firms. Instead,

I used my experience from working in the corporate world, and I read as much as I could about industry leaders. I borrowed a good idea from here and another from there. Become curious (if you aren't already) and start to look out for good ideas that will travel.

Books are a good third-hand source of knowledge. Beware of webinars and podcasts that are designed to promote the broadcaster, as the quality may vary. An interview with a leading business person may be full of gems you can adapt or replicate, or it may just be interesting.

The first books that I'd recommend you start with are as follows:

The E-Myth Revisited – Michael Gerber (2001)

This is all about how to introduce systems into a business so that everything operates more efficiently. This, in turn, increases profit whilst decreasing dependence on the business owner. A business that's less dependent on particular staff is more valuable when it comes to the sale of the business, but it also allows those individuals to take more time off to build a better work-life balance or to drive the firm onwards and upwards.

The 4-hour Work Week – Tim Ferris (2011)

This book is about deliberately building a business from scratch to earn sufficient profit for the owner to do what they want with most of their time. Whilst it isn't about adapting an existing business, there are plenty of tips that can be modified so you can work less in a business that you love.

The 12-Week Year: Get more done in 12 weeks than others do in 12 months – Brian P. Moran and Michael Lennington (2013)

Learn how to keep the momentum going on your projects so that each 12-week period is productive. I like to save the 13th week for holiday and recovery time, although I think we all deserve more than four weeks holiday per year. I'm aware that, in some countries, four weeks is aspirational, but we all work much better when we're well rested.

Profit First — Mike Michalowicz (2017)

The first two chapters of this book are enough to get you thinking differently about your business. Whilst accountants are comfortable accruing money and budgeting for future costs and taxes, most business owners are more comfortable with setting aside pots of money in different bank accounts. Even though I'm an accountant myself, I still like to sweep my cash into the different savings spaces each Friday afternoon.

Growing by Numbers — Della Hudson FCA (2020)

Whilst it might seem odd to recommend my own book, I wrote this book solely to help small-business owners scale up, so there are plenty of ideas that you can share.

There are plenty of books to help start-up businesses or leaders of larger businesses, but I found limited resources on scaling up a small business. However, this is the area where we can give most help and generate an affordable fee. Through the business advice we had given in my first accountancy firm, I collated a wealth of knowledge and resources, so I put them together in a book I could give to my clients before starting work with them.

A book with your name on is a good resource for promoting your advisory services. Ideally, you'll write your own, but that takes time, money and expertise. If you want to give copies of *Growing by Numbers* to your clients to promote your own advisory services, then we can arrange for copies to be dual branded with your logo.

Helping your clients

As well as giving ad hoc advice to your clients, you should start to build a library of helpsheets on common advice topics. Think about the questions you're commonly asked, such as these:

- Should I incorporate?
- Should I VAT register?
- How do I connect my bank to Xero?
- What's MTD?

For each question you come up with, write up the answer once or record a short video, and then keep this to hand so that you and your team can help your clients with the minimum of effort.

We'd send them to our clients with a covering email saying, "Please get in touch if you have further questions." Receiving a further request after sending free information would usually be the sign that the next advice should be chargeable.

Partner with other experts (see Chapter 9) and make sure that, if you can't do it, you know somebody who can.

Summary

- ¤ You don't have to charge for advice if you're happy that you're getting healthy compliance fees in return for your reactive advice.
- ¤ Accumulate advice ideas from your own practice.
- ¤ Look for transferable ideas from other businesses and industries.
- ¤ Read books for ideas to help your clients.
- ¤ Build a library of helpsheets and/or videos.
- ¤ Build a network of experts whom you can refer to.

9.
Working with experts

I keep saying it, but advisory isn't for everyone. I feel that I need to get this message across, as it often feels like there's a lot of pressure to provide such services. Much of that pressure comes from software companies that believe they can help, so I've tried to include some of the more useful ones in this book (see Chapter 4). There are far too many to include, so do look for your own solutions too.

Pretty much all businesses need advice, but they're not all able to pay for it. This is because they either don't have the resources or don't understand the value of such assistance. *However*, that advice doesn't need to come from their accountant.

You might be content with providing good compliance services to give a firm foundation to your clients. Perhaps you throw in a bit of advice as you go, but you don't want the fuss of offering it as a separate service (see Chapter 8). You might not have the skills or the desire to provide advisory services, and that's alright because there's an alternative.

You might want to offer only some traditional advice services, such as tax and funding. You can still help your clients to find good advice elsewhere. You can partner with business-advice experts in a number of ways.

Franchises

Entrepreneurs Circle offers business-advice franchises that you can buy into. There's a monthly workbook and discussion topic to help you run small mastermind-style events.

Action Coach is another franchise that offers group and individual coaching. It provides training and materials for you to follow.

White-labelled products

Growing by Numbers Online is my own service, and it can be white labelled for accountants to run their own courses. There are 10 prerecorded webinars, and you can either join our group coaching sessions or run your own. These are intended to be run alongside a management accounts service from the client's own accountant. We can also offer individual coaching under your umbrella.

The Gap provides a set of materials for you to generate written content and a series of webinars to support your clients and others.

Local partnerships

If you want even less involvement than this, then you can operate a simple system of referrals to your local business coach. This can be in return for a referral fee or it may be more beneficial to look at a reciprocal referral arrangement, as each of the coach's clients will require an accountant.

Summary

- You don't have to offer business-advice services yourself.
- You ought to have a route for your clients to get the advice that they need.
- Consider buying a franchise.
- Consider buying in white-labelled courses and materials.
- Consider partnering with other local advisers and coaches.

10.
Marketing advisory services

The ideal client for your advisory services may not be the same as for your accounts and tax services, so you may end up with a different client avatar (refer to The Numbers Business Online [see Appendix 1] for more information about marketing your practice generally). At Hudson Business Accountants and Advisers, we focused on marketing our advisory services, and this generated enquiries for accountancy too. As much of my current coaching and business advice is for accountants, I keep this separate from Minerva Accountants.

You may also be able to cross-sell advisory services to your existing clients. It may be as simple as making them aware of the services you offer, or you may need to demonstrate your expertise in this area.

Whether marketing internally or externally, you need to be clear on the following:

- the problems you can solve;
- the sorts of businesses you can help; and
- the services you can offer.

All your marketing should be directed at this ideal client. You may pick up some okay clients too, but keep your marketing narrow and focused, so that your ideal client feels as though you're speaking directly to them about their problems. Marketing is often compared to dating, and you certainly wouldn't write a love letter to "To whom it may concern", rather you would address it to a specific individual that you know and like.

Although every business can benefit from advice, you need to focus on those that can afford to pay. As business advice isn't a commodity service, like compliance is, you need to differentiate your expertise.

The main ways of doing this are through these:

- Speaking
- Writing
- Case studies and testimonials

Writing

Writing a book is a great way to demonstrate your expertise. However, it isn't for everybody because of the time and costs involved.

Paper or e-book

A paperback will sit on somebody's shelf until they're ready to read it. They'll see your name again and again, like it's an expensive business card. But paperbacks are expensive to produce. E-books are cheaper, but they're more easily overlooked.

Business books are unlikely to make you money through direct sales of the book itself. This is why having a clear call to action throughout the book is essential, as it's the back-end sales that are made from the content of the book that will recoup your publishing costs, and in some cases, this can be as high as 10 times the investment.

Self-publish or independent?

You're unlikely to be given an advance from a traditional publisher unless you or your book will guarantee them a high volume of sales. This leaves you with the option of self-publishing, either by doing all the work yourself or commissioning an independent publisher to publish at your expense. An independent publisher can provide you with the same high standards as more conventional publishing houses, but you'll pay their costs up front. The benefit is that you'll have control over your own intellectual property, so you can reproduce your content in any way you wish, such as in blogs, articles, webinars or podcasts.

If you choose to self-publish by doing all of the work yourself, you'll be responsible for copy-editing, proofreading, typesetting, graphic design, etc. Unless you employ individual professionals for each part of the process, there's usually a clear difference in quality. This may be sufficient for you or you may want to showcase your expertise more appropriately.

Who will write it?

Accountants may be good at writing reports, but we're not always good at telling stories that engage our audience and bring them with us on the buying journey, which is the purpose of such a book. In other words, you may not be the best person to write your book, so you may prefer to pay a ghostwriter to help you.

Dual brand Growing by Numbers

A quick and easy way to get your name on a book is to dual brand my book *Growing by Numbers*. Whilst this isn't demonstrating your personal expertise, it's the next best thing.

Other reasons to write a book

Although this chapter is about using a book to market your advisory services, there are other reasons to write a book. It can be particularly useful in helping you to get your thoughts in order and to develop the methodology you'll use to deliver your advisory services. If you write a book with this in mind, then you may choose to publish it or not.

Writing short-form content

Writing shorter articles and blogs is much simpler than crafting a whole book. These can be published on your own website, in newsletters and on social media. They may also be acceptable as advertorials in local publications.

Speaking at events

Why?

Retailers have a shop window, and customers often have the opportunity to touch and feel a retailer's products before they buy. The equivalent for service clients is to offer some (free) advice and an opportunity to get to know the expert. The difficulty with this is finding the balance between providing something useful and not giving away your most valuable knowledge.

Which events?

You can either run the event yourself for maximum publicity or speak at somebody else's event to save yourself the hassle of organising it. You may choose to do a mixture of both.

Wherever you speak, ensure the audience includes some of your ideal clients. Speaking at an event for accountants might be good for your ego, but you won't have any prospects in your audience.

Finding speakers

If you really can't speak yourself, then you may want to get one of your other expert advisers to represent you.

If you need help with public speaking or just an opportunity to brush up on it, then Alexandra Bond Burnett and Scott Johnston are both public-speaking coaches who work with accountants (see Appendix 1 for further details). You could also join Toastmasters. If you're already speaking at a good level and want to improve further still, then I'm happy to recommend the Professional Speaking Association; you may recognise some of our members from accountancy stages and video screens.

Promoting and pricing your event

Although the organiser should promote your event, you also ought to get the details out to all your networks. In order to promote the event, you'll need your subject, summary and personal profile. You'll also need a date, time and venue. A good headshot will be necessary too.

Attending such an event is a low-risk way for people to experience your expertise. If the event is free, they'll only be investing their time. The benefit of a paid event is that you'll only get people who are seriously interested in the topic and who are prepared to pay for it.

Rehearsal

A professional speaker with a new 45-minute talk will probably take one to two days to write their talk and rehearse it to an acceptable standard. As with the quality of a book, you need to decide how much effort to put in and what will be acceptable to your ideal clients.

On the day

Arrive at the venue or online in plenty of time to perform the necessary technical tests.

You may be happy with just getting the speaking exposure, or you may wish to include contact information or some sort of swag in delegate packs. We've always provided our guest speakers with a video of their talk and the contact details of the videographer in case they want it edited in any way.

Agree with your host how you want to be introduced. It's normal to provide a couple of sentences for them to read out, but this may need to be adapted to tie in with the overall event.

Also confirm with your host about their policy on 'selling from the stage'. Whilst this is usually frowned upon, for an unpaid talk, it's common to close with a call to action to contact you about X or an invitation to Y in lieu of a fee.

Video and photographs

It's easy to arrange for a professional videographer to record live seminars. The videos of my talks have always been edited to 'cup-of-tea length' segments for our website, YouTube channel and to share on social media. In the early days, it was quite useful for me to watch these back in order to identify areas for improvement. The clips themselves were also useful to share with prospective and existing clients, and the most popular one was on cash flow.

You can also use the opportunity to ask for some video testimonials on the events and on your services in general.

Repurposing content

This is about making the most of your content. The same content can be reused fairly easily; here are some suggestions:

- » Use the full content for a live talk.
- » Create a full-length recording to sell or give away.
- » Cut the video into 'cup-of-tea length' segments that people could watch later or that could be used in the same way as our helpsheets when somebody had a question. Share them on YouTube, your website and social media.

» Split each talk into about three articles for distribution to third parties, including the local paper and social media.

» Split each talk into three to six blogs, which could also be shared on social media.

» Make some of the content into helpsheets.

» Use the written and video content to promote your next event.

» Use some of the content to form the basis of your book.

Webinars

The advantages of webinars are that they're cheap, they're easy to run, and people can watch them from their own desk or home. We run two webinar series: *Better Business*, which is for accountants and bookkeepers; and *Money Matters*, which is for muggles or other business owners (see Appendix 1 for details). The latter also acts as a differentiator when promoting our accountancy services. Nobody can see if you're presenting to an audience of one or 100, and if you record the webinar, you can reuse it again and again. Learn from my mistake and do remember to press the record button! I now write this instruction at the beginning of my talk notes.

If you're shy about public speaking, you can even read from your script, but do try not to sound as though you're doing this. I usually start the webinar with a live camera on me to say hello, and then I switch to slides that I can talk over.

The downside of webinars is that there isn't an opportunity for networking or getting to know your audience.

Third-party evidence

Testimonials and case studies act as third-party evidence of your expertise. These can be included on your website, social media and other marketing sites. In some cases, a good case study may be worth publishing in your local or business press. Public relations (PR) companies can help to get your business story in front of people. It was described to me that journalists take the news and write the story, whereas content writers have to find your story and make it newsworthy. A good PR article is much more than content, as you need an expert with the right connections to get it into the press publications that are relevant to you. We use PR the Write Way for all our work (see Appendix 1 for website details).

De-risking your services

These samples of your expertise help to reduce the risk associated with the buying decision for your clients. Another way to do this is to include a guarantee. Whilst this might feel a little risky, most of us would probably offer a refund if a client wasn't satisfied with our services. Your contract can offer a guarantee, provided that the client has turned up for all sessions and implemented the actions as agreed. If these still don't have the expected benefits, then you can offer a refund or an additional session to make up the shortfall.

Summary

- ¤ Writing a book can help with both marketing your services and deciding on your methodology.
- ¤ Articles and blogs are easier to write than a whole book.
- ¤ Speaking is another excellent way of demonstrating your expertise.
- ¤ Repurpose your content for maximum effect.
- ¤ Include third-party evidence and case studies.
- ¤ Consider offering a guarantee.

PART 2

WHAT ADVISORY SERVICES TO PROVIDE

Part 2 of this book will provide some ideas on what to include in your advisory sessions. There's a chapter on each of the main advisory areas that we cover, but you may prefer to cover only a few of these or there may be others you can add. You can also provide advisory services through introductions to third parties.

It's important that you develop your own systems and style, but these are some ideas you can use until you find your own way. I'd also love to hear of other things that have worked for you.

11.
Clarifying the vision & values

Before we accountants can start any work with a client, even compliance, we need to understand their vision for their business. For owner-managed businesses, we go deeper and clarify the owner's vision for their life, so that we can understand how their business fits into this.

There are several ways to encourage people to think about their vision. Where there's more than one owner/director, then it's worth getting them to do these exercises separately to see where the business can help to move each of them towards their personal goals.

The goals can usually be divided into one of three categories:

1. Increased profitability now
2. Increased business valuation, with a view to a sale now or in the future
3. A better work-life balance, requiring less time in the business

Most of the same business advice can be used to support all three goals, but with a different emphasis for each. An efficient, systemised business with the right work, the right team and the right prices should be profitable, saleable and not overly dependent on the owner.

I once ran a strategic-planning day for a struggling company with four director-shareholders. As usual, we started with a very brief look at their personal goals. Between the four of them, they had three very different goals that were influencing what they each wanted the business to do for them. It was no surprise that they weren't able to pull together in the same direction, as they all had a different idea of where 'forward' was.

One was supposed to be retiring, but he was unable to get himself out of the business; one wanted to work remotely so that he could spend more time sailing; and two wanted more profit to pay for their large house with accompanying mortgage.

As you'll see throughout this book, the actions are often the same for multiple goals, so we were able to come up with a strategy that sorted out two of the goals very well and helped with the third one too.

Every now and then, I wonder what would have happened to their business if they'd continued to pull in different directions.

Helping clients identify their goals

There are a number of methods you can use to help your clients think about their goals. Different techniques will suit some different personalities better than others. Sometimes, people get a little bit stuck on where to start, so you may need to tease it out of them and help them to organise their ideas. We usually look at a five-year horizon for planning, as it's rarely worth trying to make detailed plans any further ahead, but there's nothing wrong with having a longer-term goal.

Ideal day

Ask your client to describe their ideal day. Not just the work day but the whole day. Where do they live and with whom, and what time do they start work? Then ask what sort of activities they do at work. This will probably be the things they enjoy most or that they consider the most profitable. What time do they finish work and how do they spend their evenings?

Mood board or Pinterest

Making use of a mood board or Pinterest works well for more visual people. They can collate ideas on how they want their life and their business to look and feel once they've achieved their goals. The pictures will give you a clue as to what those goals are.

Dreams-and-desires folder

My father used to work with reformed drug addicts. As well as helping them to move forwards into work or training, part of what he did was to give them something more positive to look forward to if ever they felt themselves getting pulled back towards their old lifestyle.

Collate things that represent your future goals; it can be a good idea to keep them together in a folder. I had an estate agent's printout of a beautiful house with a pool and views to die for, which represented financial success as well as a home for me. I also had a brochure for a local chauffeur company, as I wanted to take life a bit easier. On the other hand, I also had a training plan for an ironman, which I finally got to use in 2017!

Other symbols

When my kids were smaller, I had a jar of marbles on my desk next to my monitor, which was a tip from another accounting guru. As I had set up my business to spend quality time with my kids, each marble represented one of the weeks remaining until my eldest would head off to university. Each Sunday evening or Monday morning, I'd remove one marble, try to think of what quality time we had spent together over the past week and then plan something for the next week.

These days, I'm building a business that will enable me to work from anywhere in the world. My symbols are a shell from a beach in Spain and a 30-second video-and-audio clip of waves on a beach. Between them, they provide me with something visual, audible and tactile. They're not the whole story but are a useful reminder.

There are all sorts of other methods to help people identify their vision.

Summarise the vision

Once you have the detailed picture, try to get the personal vision down to a single simple sentence. This isn't the business vision but what the owner(s) want to get out of it. For my first business, I wanted "interesting, professional work that fitted around family life".

Values

As well as understanding the vision, it's important to understand the owner's values. The vision is what they want, and the values are how they'll get there.

Before our meeting with an owner, we usually provide a sheet of values that might be perceived as positive, negative or neutral. The owner has to highlight all those they agree with and then circle the three that appeal most. They also have to cross out any that they don't like. Finally, they're encouraged to add other values (which we then add to our main list for the next group).

Everybody has difficulty getting down to just three, but as with many of these exercises, it's about the thought process as much as the outcome.

We discuss the chosen values with the owners to clarify what the selected words mean to them, as well as those that almost made the final three.

When running values sessions for a business or a team within a business, you can try brainstorming. Brainstorming is a great way to liberate people to say what they think, and it can stimulate some healthy debate. When carrying out group sessions like this, it's important that you, the facilitator, encourage everybody to have a say. Introverts may be less keen to shout out, but they may be happy to write extra words onto sticky notes or a flipchart, either as part of the main session or throughout the day before they're discussed later.

Logistics

We'd run a vision-and-values session over a short day (10am–3pm), with some exercises prepared in advance.

These sessions are best conducted off site to minimise interruptions.

For a face-to-face session, it's worth including lunch and a break that's short enough to catch up on anything urgent but not long enough to get dragged back into the main business. If you carry out long sessions like this online, then you'll probably need a 10-minute comfort break once an hour.

Summary

- ☐ Start with the vision before you begin offering advice.

- ☐ There are many ways to capture this vision.

- ☐ Identify the values of the owner(s) and the business, so that everybody understands how they want to do business.

12.
Changing the cash flow

Cash is a key area in which accountants can offer advice. It's a pain point in many organisations, and there are a number of tools that can help your clients. This is the area that probably keeps most business owners awake at night, so you can clearly offer value if you can get this part of their business under control.

Management accounts and forecasts

As this is more traditional work, I've already covered it in detail in Chapter 3.

Reducing debtor days

There are several things you can advise your clients to do to help reduce debtor days (see Appendix 1 for the website details of all organisations and software mentioned here):

- **Terms and conditions** – You can ensure that your clients have appropriate terms and conditions, including credit periods that are as short as is practical. If they need help writing these, then you can refer them to legal partners or template resources, such as those provided to members of the Federation of Small Businesses (FSB) or purchased from Simply-Docs.

- **Credit control procedures** – You can assist your clients with putting together appropriate credit control procedures. These processes can then be automated or followed manually, or perhaps both. You can explain the importance of having the right paperwork signed off in plenty of time, including purchase order numbers and variation orders for any subsequent changes.
- **Credit checks** – You can help your clients to check out their own customers, so they only offer credit where appropriate.
- **Satago** – This is a software and finance company that also provides a specific training programme to help you help your clients. With their assistance, you can offer five levels of support:
  - Credit control checks
  - Credit control health checks
  - Software for credit control, with automated reminders and analysis
  - An outsourced credit control function
  - Invoice financing for the full company or selected invoices/customers
- **Chaser** – This is a software company that delivers automated chasing emails. These differ from Satago's reminders in that you have the ability to edit the list before it's sent.
- **Outsourced credit control** – You may wish to offer this as a service or to work with a local company that does this. You may already have staff who can provide this service, or you may need to recruit in order to support credit control as an additional income stream.

- **Settlement discounts** – You can work out the costs and benefits of offering settlement discounts or charging interest on overdue payments.

- **Xero** – This software has the ability to send standard reminders based on editable templates. These don't have the full functionality of Chaser or Satago, but they'll serve the smallest clients. There's often resistance to automated chasing, but the first emails can be worded simply to check that the invoice has been received and everything has been approved for payment, or to ask the client if they have any queries. Xero also allows the user to see when invoices have been seen, so there are no more excuses of "We haven't received it."

- **Faster payments** – Such faster payments are now possible using GoCardless for direct debits, and iwocaPay or Stripe buttons can be added to invoices for instant card payments and/or short-term credit for customers. Zettle by PayPal and Square both offer small card readers that can be used by customers to take payments on site or in taxis.

- **Court involvement** – As a last resort, customers sometimes need to get the courts involved, so you can advise on the process for doing this themselves through the small claims court, or you can introduce them to your legal contacts or a debt-recovery service.

Reducing lock-up in stock

We can show the impact of receiving faster deliveries from suppliers in exchange for losing bulk discounts. We can also help to identify the most appropriate volumes to hold in stock and explain why "If you build it, [they] will come" (*Field of Dreams*, 1989) isn't always the best policy for purchasing stock.

We can help to identify slow-moving stock, pinpoint what the best-selling products are and suggest useful cross-sales.

Supplier payments

Delaying supplier payments is a way to increase cash balances, but they should always be agreed with the supplier and not breach the agreed terms. There may also be a moral duty to support small companies that don't have access to huge funds to buffer late payments.

Invoice financing

This is available through Satago and many banks. It can be useful for a short-term cash crisis or project, but it's less suitable for long-term funding.

Referrals to appropriate banks

We can ensure that our clients have access to appropriate banks. The services and fees of challenger banks vs traditional banks can be very different.

Summary

- ¤ Use management accounts and cash-flow forecasting.
- ¤ Increase cash by managing debtors.
- ¤ Increase cash by monitoring stock.
- ¤ Increase cash by managing supplier payments.
- ¤ Use credit control software.
- ¤ Make legal referrals where needed.
- ¤ Refer clients to the right bank for them.

13.
Changing the pricing

Changing the pricing is the single best way to increase profit, as every pound added to the price goes straight to profit. This is another key area for getting started in advisory.

Every business needs to make a certain amount of money to cover direct costs, wages, other overheads and an amount for the owner(s). Small-business owners take more risks than a normal employee, so they should earn at least the equivalent of a salary. They may also work longer hours, and this should also be taken into account in their remuneration; far too many business owners earn less than minimum wage due to the long hours they work.

Proper pricing is essential for four reasons:

1. **Financial freedom** – This is the obvious one. If the owner were to substitute an employee doing the same work at a commercial salary, would there still be any profit? If not, this is self-employment rather than a business. It may be a step on the way to growing an independent business, but we can help our clients to get beyond that stage faster.

2. **Quality and pride** – In order to provide a service or product of which the owner can be proud, then they need to be able to put in sufficient time and resources to carry out the work required. Whilst money may be an

important motivator, most small-business owners start with a dream of providing a good-quality product or service. Poor pricing may force them to rush to complete a job because it's just haemorrhaging cash and time.

3. **Time freedom** – If they don't charge enough to pay someone to do the work, it's often the business owner who puts in the extra hours to complete the job. Proper pricing will pay for time – either personal time or time to grow their business.

4. **To cover growing salary and overhead bills** – Hopefully, you've advised them how much to allow for this from the start. If they set up with 'I'm working from home with no costs' type of prices, then before they can start to scale up, they may need to spend time replacing all their customers with others who can/will pay full price.

Many business owners are too scared to increase their prices because they worry that they'll lose clients who can't or won't pay the necessary fee. We can help them with this by working out the right prices, calculating the risks, and providing scripts or templates to help them notify existing clients of their amended prices.

Issues to consider when advising your clients on correct pricing

Market price and where they sit in the market

When first setting up in business, prices are usually based broadly in line with competitors, as if this were the market price. Helping your client to differentiate their product(s) or service(s) can justify a very different price.

> Babycham was just another perry (pear cider) before its marketing was changed to focus on women. It was the first drink targeted at women in this way. The name suggests something more like champagne than the pear cider it actually is. Its prices were increased substantially to move it into the luxury end of the market.

Where do your clients really sit in their market and can marketing help them to do what they do better?

The value they provide to their customers

Value pricing is when you set your prices based on the value of the benefit to your customer. If a boiler fails in the middle of winter, then the acceptable price of installing a new boiler will be significantly higher than doing so in the summer.

Cost-based pricing

This is where prices are based on the cost of providing the product or service (including a share of overheads and a profit element).

Cost-based pricing is normal in retail, where products are bought in at one price and then sold on for the cost plus a percentage mark-up.

This used to be normal for professional services, such as the hourly charging of traditional accountants and solicitors, with no reward for efficiency or automation. Carrying out a similar job will be faster the second time, so it's unfair to penalise one client for the learning curve or to undercharge another. More professionals are now moving to fixed fees to remove the uncertainty for clients. These fixed fees are still usually based loosely on the expected number of hours.

It's clear that small businesses cannot compete on price against the big corporations that "Pile 'em high, sell 'em cheap" (Jack

Cohen, founder of Tesco). These companies have purchasing power and economies of scale that small businesses can't hope to match. They also probably can't compete with the small businesses based at home, which have minimal overheads. Competitor businesses below the VAT threshold can sell to both the public and non-VAT registered clients who cannot reclaim VAT without needing to add the 20% VAT premium.

Price and quality

What your clients can compete on is quality and/or value for money.

How long does it take and how much does it cost your client to do a fairly standard job of average quality? How much could they charge for that particular job?

Now consider how much more it would take to provide the kind of job with added wow factor. How much could they charge now? How much extra would it cost?

When new clients came to me and complained that they weren't getting the kind of service they wanted from their accountant, the first thing I did was to ask how much they were paying. My response was usually along the lines of, "How can you expect the service you describe for that fee?"

It's rare to get extraordinary value at the cheap end of the market. The most extreme example was somebody who was paying £50 per year to a family friend and expected monthly management accounts for that price – a job we'd price at a few thousand pounds! As she was self-employed, that price wasn't realistic for her, but neither was her need for monthly accounts. We agreed on a realistic price and service for her business, and we told her which key numbers to monitor each month.

Increasing prices

Even in retail, if you can add value in some way, you can often charge a premium. Consider the price you'd pay for a basket of toiletries that are beautifully packaged as a gift compared to the price you'd pay for almost identical toiletries sold separately and purchased as part of your weekly shop. (Adding value yourself is also a good hint for Christmas presents when you're feeling hard up).

Many people worry that they may lose business by putting up their prices, but let me show you an example:

If you have 100 sales of £1,000 each and an associated cost per item of £500 (so £500 profit per item), you might choose to increase your prices by 10% to £1,100.

Now, instead of an income of £100,000 and profit of £50,000, you'd have an income of £110,000 and profit of £60,000.

If you lose 10% of your clients through this 10% price increase, you'd still have 90 clients paying £1,100 each, an income of £99,000 and profit of £54,000. You've increased your profit by £4,000 whilst having more time to do a good job for fewer clients.

With this example, you could afford to lose 17% of your customers and still make the same profit, but you'd be ahead on the processing costs because you're handling fewer transactions.

Use your numerical skills to work out the equivalent numbers for your clients. What proportion of their clients can they afford to lose and still break even?

As an added bonus, the most price-sensitive customers are probably those who cause the most hassle. Your client will have their own example of where they've been squeezed on profit, and the customer was still not satisfied or the product wasn't up to standard.

Negotiating prices

When we first set up in business, we're often feeling our way on pricing. After a while, we know what we're worth, although people sometimes still try to negotiate beyond this. Your client may have legacy prices with older customers that need to be addressed.

Once you've worked out the correct prices, you can help your client to stand firm on these in a way that they probably couldn't do alone. My shoulders are broad, and I'm quite happy for clients to blame me – "My accountant wouldn't allow that!" – when they're asked for discounts.

Why do professionals and tradies charge by the hour? It's usually because they've always done it that way, but if it's a fairly standard job (obviously, this doesn't apply to every job) where they know roughly the time it'll take, then it gives the customer more certainty if they're quoted a fixed fee rather than an hourly rate.

Presenting prices

There's been a great deal of research showing that if you present three models with increasing price and quality, people will often avoid the cheapest, as they don't wish to be seen as being cheap.

Your client could have bronze, silver and gold packages. Or perhaps something a little more creative, as long as there's an indication of an increase in value along with the increase in prices.

Warning

If your client increases their prices without delivering value for money, then they'll end up losing business and reputation. Overpricing is a short-term solution, and it may backfire if they need any sort of repeat business or referrals.

For instance, plumbers charging too much of a premium during the busy winter period may find that they're not called in for the annual maintenance or anything else. However, if they get their pricing right, plumbing businesses can go back through all their callouts and use them to schedule maintenance visits over the quieter summer period.

> My favourite client testimonial is this: "You are more expensive than [another local accountant], but much easier to deal with."
>
> I like it because it shows that I got our pricing right on this one, and the client appreciated that we were giving value for money. I used this quote in our marketing for a while.

Annual increases

Don't forget that costs usually go up. Make time to review your clients' prices each year to ensure that they're continuing to make the same profit, but are also in line with where they sit in the market. They should probably have a standard inflationary price increase to cover their own costs, and it's easier to do this on an annual basis than to have a large price hike every few years.

Overcharging or underservicing?

> Have you ever been sitting in a restaurant whilst waiting for your meal and fancied another drink? This happened to me recently, and the server was nowhere to be seen, so I was left sitting there, thirsty, and noticing the lack of service and the long wait for food.

Although it may sometimes be irritating to be cross-sold extras, it was probably more infuriating to be without the drink I wanted, which also led me to notice faults that I'd otherwise have overlooked. As well as losing out on an extra sale that would have added about 21% to my bill, the restaurant had an unhappy customer who may well go elsewhere next time.

You don't need a hard sell, but do ensure that your clients are aware of any additional services that you think may be of use to them.

How to get rid of unprofitable customers

Once a year, it's a good idea to evaluate the customers and/or products of each of your clients. Customers and products that were profitable and fitted the business objectives last year may no longer be ideal.

Help your client to triage their products, services, regions, etc. into the following:

- The perfect product/customer, which is profitable and easy to work with.
- A pretty good product/customer, for the same reasons.
- Those products/customers that aren't quite there, but with a bit of work would be A or B. This might mean tightening up on how work is carried out, amending production processes or adjusting prices to improve profitability.
- Those products/customers that don't suit their current profile. Perhaps they were lovely people or products, but are now unprofitable or a bad fit for your client's business.

There are two actions to come out of this triage:

1. Making the necessary changes to improve Cs such that they become As or Bs.
2. Getting rid of D products/customers.

One of our clients was running a professional services company. When I was first called in, he was working long hours, seven days a week. He was aware, in theory, of the need to move unprofitable clients on, but he wasn't quite sure how to do it professionally.

This is what we did:

- His financial controller provided an analysis of the criteria for a profitable client, so we were able to come up with the list quite objectively.
- We discussed how his business had moved on and why they were no longer able to look after those clients profitably if he wanted to provide their usual high levels of service.
- We came up with a script he could use as a basis for the individual conversations.
- Where possible, he identified other companies that would provide the basic service at an affordable price.
- He contacted each client and explained that the business was no longer able to provide them with a good-quality basic service at an affordable price, and he made the introduction to the new agent.

As a result, the business lost 22% of its work, which freed up a lot of the owner's time. It also lost 6% of its profit, but this was quickly replaced because there was now time to manage the enquiries from ideal clients.

Avoiding pitfalls

If you're worried about making a generic price increase or don't know what you're worth, then you can phase in an increase by starting with new business. Then, just increase prices for a few existing products or customers each month.

Don't be afraid of losing poor customers.

These are the numbers to watch:

- The criteria/size of your ideal client
- The minimum fee, if it's appropriate to set one
- The average income per client/product
- The profitability per client / product / geographical market

Summary

- ¤ Your client is in business to make money, not to provide a charitable service.
- ¤ There's nothing wrong with them being paid what they're worth.
- ¤ They need to charge enough to provide the level of service that they're comfortable with. Increasing prices will minimise overservicing issues.
- ¤ Quality commands a higher fee, but do make sure that they fulfil their promises.
- ¤ Try bundling products and services into packages to help with pricing and cross-selling.
- ¤ Increase all prices annually by default.
- ¤ Don't be afraid to increase prices if they're too low; your client can blame their accountant.

14.
Changing the time

If only we could all find more time, we could get so much more done. Unfortunately, we can't create more time, so we have to focus on priorities instead.

You can work with your clients on two types of time management: personal time management and how they can manage their team to get the most out of them.

Balanced 10

Everybody wants a good work-life balance, although we might all have different definitions of what that is. Life outside of work may consist of any number of things, but I like to use the analogy of a wheel with 10 spokes. If the spokes are all different lengths, then you have a wonky wheel and you're probably not going anywhere.

> I chose to run my first practice on 25 hours per week, a normal school week, to fit around my small children. Those small children are now teenagers, and I'm pleased that I had the privilege of spending time with them whilst they were growing up. I still run my current business on 25 hours per week because, frankly, I believe I'm worth it. I'm also more productive over five shorter days.

Feel free to create your own wheel that's based on the things you and your clients hold dear, but here are the 10 areas of life that we like to look at:

1. **Work** – The rest of this book is focused on improving this.

2. **Family and friends** – How much *quality* time do you spend with them whilst awake? Do you try to be home for bath time and bed time with little ones, or do you aim for better chunks of time and activity with teenagers or adult friends? Do you need shorter working hours or more flexibility?

3. **Health** – Are you eating, drinking and sleeping properly? How are your weight and fitness? Do you take regular exercise? If not, then how do we build these good habits into your life, one at a time?

4. **Finance** – Your income probably comes from your business, but you also need to consider your outgoings. Living within your means is much less stressful than the other way around, as Charles Dickens' Mr Micawber (*David Copperfield*) knew well: "Annual income 20 pounds, annual expenditure 19 [pounds] 19 [shillings] and six [pence], result happiness. Annual income 20 pounds, annual expenditure 20 [pounds] and six [pence], result misery." For small-business owners, it's important to consider personal expenses and investments.

5. **Self-image** – Many of us identify ourselves with our work or our business. Have you ever introduced yourself to a group of strangers by saying, "I'm an accountant"? Our identity is often wrapped up in what we do, so a bad period in our business may destroy our self-worth. Remember that what you do is (or should be) just a small part of who you are.

6. **Personal growth** – It's good to do something to keep improving ourselves. If you like to read self-improvement books, then do make sure that you do something as a result of what you've read. The same goes for this book. Whilst I'm pleased that you've bought this book, my real reward comes when I hear of the changes and improvements you've made after reading it. I like to read, and as I lived in many places around the world whilst I was growing up, I find languages easy to learn. At the moment, I'm taking Spanish lessons, which aren't just an area of self-improvement: they require just enough concentration that they force me to stop thinking about work. I also take singing lessons for the same reason.

7. **Spirituality or community** – This is the idea of something bigger than us. Do you give back to your community in some way? This might be time, money or expertise. Are you doing something to make the world a better place?

8. **Love** – We all need this in our life. Whether this comes from a special individual, our family or a pet, I think we're all better when we have somebody who loves us unconditionally. Somebody who will support us on our bad days and remind us that we still have value.

9. **Recreation** – Many business owners become workaholics because they both love what they do and don't have any interests outside their business. If possible, find something completely unrelated to do in your leisure time. I do triathlons, which overlaps with health and fitness, as well as getting me speaking to lots of non-accountants. It's a great sport, and with three disciplines, there's all sorts of data to analyse and improve on.

10. **Environment** – Of course, we do have a responsibility towards the global environment, but I'm also keen that we create a home and business environment that improves our personal quality of life. I find light and space relaxing at home, but you may find comfort from objects that I'd consider clutter. There's no single right answer, though you should improve your own space to enhance your life.

Have as many spokes to your wheel as you like, and adapt the different areas to cover your life priorities. Although I mainly use this with business owners to establish what they want out of their life and business, it can also be useful for managers to carry out a similar exercise with their team.

Time management

As any time management guru will point out, we all have exactly the same number of hours, but we all prioritise them differently. I have a meme, which I don't know the source of, but it sums this up well: "'I don't have enough time' is the adult equivalent of 'the dog ate my homework'." For the most part, we can prioritise our time to do the things we care about most. This mainly relies on self-discipline, but there are some useful techniques that may help, which I've detailed in the following sections.

Procrastination

Confession time: I'm a procrastinator.

I've read all sorts of books on the topic because reading is a great way of procrastinating!

There's a Bing Crosby song, 'Busy Doing Nothing', the lyrics of which pretty much sum me up. Procrastination isn't laziness, but misdirected effort. I'd love to offer a solution to all my fellow procrastinators, but I really don't have a clue, so please send me all your top tips.

Pomodoro technique

For this, you'll need a timer. The idea is to focus on a task for a period of time rather than keeping going to complete a longer job. You set a timer for just 25 minutes, work intensely for that relatively short period of time, and then you take a five-minute break.

You repeat this for two hours and then take a longer break.

I love this technique, as it does help a little with my natural tendency to procrastinate. I can't work at this rate for the whole day, but a couple of hours of good-quality work means that I can achieve something.

This doesn't really work when giving business advice, which needs to be more thoughtful, but it's useful for helping you and your clients to achieve more in other areas of business.

Chunking

Switching between different tasks can be counterproductive. I like to sort my work into different types of task: accounts review, creating short marketing content, longer writing sessions for things such as this book, high-energy coaching sessions and recording videos for my online courses. I'll also lump all my admin bits and pieces together to do on the same day, assuming they're not urgent, of course. This has the benefit of clearing lots of small items off my to-do list, and it gives me a lot of satisfaction compared to the slog of some of my bigger projects.

Default diary (time blocking)

This takes the chunking a bit further by providing a set time each week to do each type of task. It may take a while to get the right default, and it may need updating every now and again. I like to do my introverted tasks in the mornings, so my diary for mornings is usually this:

- » Monday – admin
- » Tuesday – writing a book or recording videos
- » Wednesday – work for Minerva Accountants
- » Thursday – writing marketing and other short content
- » Friday – continuous professional development (CPD) or other business improvements

I then do my people-related things in the afternoons, with telephone coaching sessions and other meetings.

You need to allow for some flexibility. My diary is easily upset by preparing and rehearsing a talk for a conference, which can take a couple of days, or by a writing deadline.

When I ran my first practice, I made Tuesdays and Thursdays my networking and meeting days so I could spend the other three days focused on work. As an introvert, this also provided me with quieter office days to recover from the people-filled days. If you're an introvert, you'll need to manage your energy as much as your time. Having a default diary is a way of prioritising time for your work and time for your clients, and it helps to minimise interruptions.

Once your client has established their default diary, these uninterruptable periods need to be blocked out as busy.

Time blocking

Time blocking is about getting every task into its own block of time in your diary. It's very common to underestimate how long each job will take. This is where limited use of timesheets can help to record exactly how long tasks take. The idea is to avoid interruptions until you reach the allocated time to deal with them.

When there's a fixed amount of time to complete a task or a limited set of tasks, this reduces procrastination and delays in starting, as well as discouraging perfectionism.

Plate spinning

Too often, we're trying to keep too many plates spinning at the same time. By allocating time in the diary for every task, it's easier to see whether the problem is too much work or poor time management.

Learn to say no

Stand in front of a mirror and repeat after me, "No." You can rehearse this with your clients. The idea is for them to practise saying it aloud.

No explanation needs to be given. Just one simple word. Of course, we do usually offer a reason, but that's a courtesy and to soften the rejection. Almost all of us need to practise saying no. Stand by your no. Don't be talked out of your no, as you know best what you can and can't do. Just keep saying no like a broken record or a small, whining child.

Assertiveness training may help with this.

Avoiding interruptions

Others have written about this extensively, so here are my top tips:

» Turn off notifications (email, phone and any other messages).

» Use an answering service to filter calls.

» Don't give everybody your mobile number! You can use a Voice over Internet Protocol (VoIP) number to divert calls to an answering service or have a second mobile.

» Turn your phone off sometimes – you don't have to answer every call immediately.

» Consider having a separate email address that can be managed by a PA, or having a generic email address that can be managed by the team.

» If you don't have a PA, then use Calendly or a similar app to organise meetings.

» Don't be available 24/7. Use a default diary to manage when you will take calls and answer emails. Few businesses are emergency services, so it should be possible to clear blocks of two hours at a time for focused work.

» Do make time to be available to others, but it doesn't need to be all the time.

The four Ds for filtering emails, etc. are these:

1. **Do it now** if it'll take less than three minutes, and then you don't need to touch the task again.

2. **Ditch it** if it isn't essential to the business. If you're busy, then 'nice to have' just isn't enough.

3. **Delegate it** to a member of staff, automate it, outsource it or call in an expert who will be better at doing it as well as faster.

4. **Defer it.** If it needs to be done, but not yet, then add it to your to-do list or your ideas list.

Team working

The best teams are greater than the sum of their parts. A team of six, all working and communicating together, can produce the work of seven to eight individuals. This is the ideal.

The best way to do this is to have a diverse but complementary team. Personality profiling can help to ensure you have such a team.

Some key things that can help to improve team working are discussed in the following sections.

Personality profiling (also useful with key customers)

I use DiSC profiling, but there are many other ways of analysing your team and how they each like to work, such as Myers-Briggs. These systems, along with some discussion (because nobody is 100% like the model), will help managers to get the best out of their team and find the best way for the team to communicate with each other. They're often used as part of the recruitment process, but it's important everybody understands them and their limitations.

Personality profiles can also work well to help businesses understand their key customers in order to optimise those relationships.

We use Smart Support for Business (see Appendix 1 for website details) to do these DiSC reports and training, but you may have a local expert.

Appraisals

Appraisals are a time to take stock. Business is busy, so it's important for managers to sit down with their team to ensure that the values and ambitions of the business, the manager and other team members are all aligned. There should be no big surprises in an appraisal, as ideally, all issues should be dealt with as they arise. The purpose is to review past performance from both the employee's and employer's perspective, and then to plan the next 6–12 months, or whatever the frequency of the appraisals is. This is the time to share detailed changes in the business and job roles, plus any training required.

For businesses that are new to appraisals or uncomfortable with the process, then I can recommend Joanne Wharam of Smart Support for Business (see Appendix 1 for website details) to run these for you and your clients.

Training

Training is investing in the team in the same way we would update software and maintain machinery to keep them operating at their best. Obviously, people need more than just training! Many businesses are loath to invest in training their team members in case they use that qualification to move on, but if they're recognising the financial progress of team members and nurturing them in other ways, then there will be less incentive for them to look for another job.

Coaching

Coaching is a particular form of training, and it's useful for employees as well as for business owners. Leadership coaching can develop skills in those responsible for teams. All too often, managers don't receive this sort of training until they're already in position, and it's a reactive choice after mistakes have been made. If you aren't a business coach, then partner with somebody who can help with this.

Succession planning

Always encourage business leaders to think ahead about the people they need in their organisation as it grows. Training up a successor means that the business is less dependent on the current incumbent in any position, should they choose to move on. It also means they have excess talent to cover holidays, sickness and business expansion.

Start with the current organisation chart and identify the skills required for each role. You can also help the owner to look at the future organisation chart in the business plan, so as to prepare for changes. Identify any skills gaps between the current team and their current and/or future skills requirements. Next, put in place the appropriate training, coaching or mentoring to bridge these gaps.

Summary

¤   There are two aspects of management: personal time management and team management. Both require well-balanced individuals, so start with the Balanced 10 exercise or your own version.

¤   The time management techniques you can use are the Pomodoro technique, time chunking, time blocking, default diary, assertiveness training and self-discipline.

¤   Team management can be improved through personality profiling, appraisals, training, coaching and succession planning.

15.
Changing the efficiency

This is my favourite area for finding improvements, as it hits every single personal ambition of business owners. Operating more efficiently increases profitability, it frees up time for the business owners to have a better work-life balance, and it also increases the value of the business for those thinking about exiting.

Hopefully, the business owner(s) have been creating systems for all the regular processes within their business from day one, but this often doesn't happen. You can start out with some checklists and templates for them to use whilst you help to document proper procedures for them and their staff. The procedures will evolve constantly as the business grows and they discover better ways of doing things. In a growing business, the written procedures will need to be reviewed continually if they're to reflect what's actually happening for more than a few months at a time.

Start by documenting the existing processes and then move on to looking for improvements to make.

Pros of systemising

Systemising a business will give you some or all of the following benefits:

- Work will be carried out to a similar (high) standard each and every time.

- Training employees will be simpler.
- Tasks can be delegated to the existing team.
- The automation of processes will be more straightforward.
- The business will be less dependent on the owner or any key person, so it's more saleable.
- The owner can be confident enough to take a holiday.
- Everyone will be able to carry out more work in the same time, as they won't need to reinvent the wheel each time, therefore increasing profit.

Cons of systemising

There are no real cons of having a properly systemised business, apart from the time it takes to keep the documentation up to date. This is where you and your team can help with an annual systems review.

Jobs that can be systemised

The following are my recommendations for the types of job, by industry, that can successfully be systemised:

- **Professional services** – Common pieces of work from the initial briefing to sign off and invoicing, booking travel, expense claims, leave requests, recruitment and training, and onboarding new clients.
- **Shops** – Cashing up, locking up, stocktaking, reordering, dealing with customer returns and banking cash (or moving to cashless systems).
- **Restaurants** – Food handling, laying up, meet and greet, dealing with delays and other complaint handling, food ordering, and stock control.

- **Trades** – Answering phones and taking messages, handling client enquiries, diary booking, quotes and invoices, and chasing payment.
- **Marketing** – Creating and distributing content in a number of formats.
- **General admin** – For all types of business.

As an outsider, it's often easier for you to spot business efficiencies than for the business owner, who is much closer to the operations. How many times have you visited a shop or restaurant and spotted inefficiencies that could easily be rectified? Even my kids do this.

How you can systemise

The following 11-step process is an outline of how you can systemise your own business and then each of your clients' businesses:

1. Read Michael Gerber's (2001) book *The E-Myth Revisited* for a detailed systemisation method, from which I gained some pointers that I've used alongside my own experience in developing my system.

2. The Pareto principle, sometimes known as 'the 80:20 rule', demonstrates that 80% of the profit comes from 20% of the products/customers. Similarly, 20% of your processes control 80% of your work. This means you should focus on those core processes first: the ones that support the majority of the customers or products. Getting these right will have the most impact on the efficiency and profitability of the business.

3. Map out the process with sticky notes attached to wallpaper or rolls of drawing paper. There are online tools to do this too, but this is one of the few processes where I prefer paper, as it's easy to see and share with a small team around a table. Sticky notes can be moved around as you start to fill in more detail about the existing system.

4. Write this up as the existing procedure, warts and all, so that you have a base that at least sort of works. (Hint: Take a photograph of the process and/or fix the notes on with sticky tape before you move the main paper).

5. Now repeat the mapping and include any improvements. Seek to make the processes more efficient and to eliminate rework or poor customer service, which leads to costly (time or money) rectification.

6. Write up this improved procedure.

7. Complete the documented task yourself by following the procedure only.

8. Add whatever extra steps you need.

9. Get somebody else to complete the task by following the procedure.

10. Add whatever extra steps you need.

11. Review the process regularly to do the following:

   - Make sure it's working.
   - Add any variations that you hadn't originally identified.
   - Eliminate bottlenecks.
   - Improve the process, because quality assurance should be a process of continuous improvement.

The checklists that might have served the business initially now need to be developed into procedures that can be used for training employees. Moving from delegating individual jobs to handing over whole areas of workflow will use these procedures to preserve consistency and quality.

One of our clients was running a professional services company. When I was first called in, he was working long hours, seven days a week. He had successfully recruited a competent team, and they were capable of handling more, but he was often the bottleneck because they needed his expertise. We switched his focus away from doing the work himself to spending slightly longer writing more how-to guides on the common issues. Soon, the team were starting to write their own how-to guides. As each person found a better way of doing part of the job, they shared it with the rest of the team.

***

Another client of mine was running an accountancy business. His aim was to work himself out of the business, ready for retirement, so we looked for areas where he was a bottleneck. Invoicing was one of those areas because he was the only one who knew what needed to be invoiced. We agreed this:

- All annual fees would be subject to the same annual % increase, so that the team could raise draft invoices.
- Due to having a known fixed fee, each client could spread their payment over 12 months, which was easier for both their cash flow and for the firm's.
- Any ad hoc work would be invoiced as it was completed, rather than added to the annual bill, so that there would be less chance of a client querying this, and not only would it be invoiced sooner but also there would be fewer queries, so it would be paid faster.
- Clients would be encouraged to pay by direct debit to reduce admin costs for both the client and the firm.

Systemise, automate and delegate

Use the documented procedures to automate as much as possible. Where it isn't possible or cost-effective to automate, then delegate to the cheapest person available.

Who can help you

We provide coaching, training and retreats for business owners.

You might use an independent consultant to help map and improve your processes, or to act as a facilitator in the mapping, a source of new ideas and an extra pair of hands.

Implementing new procedures

Documenting the ever-changing systems in a growing business could become a full-time role, but the important thing is to communicate these changes with the team. Not only will they have to follow these procedures, but they may also have good ideas on how to improve them. Involving the team at an early stage will not just allow you to get their ideas, but in addition, will help to get their buy in to any resulting changes.

Summary

- ¤ Mapping the existing systems is as important for maintaining consistent standards as it is for growth.
- ¤ System maps are also the starting point of a continuous improvement process, which will serve to either improve the individual system or systemise more processes. These are both ways to enhance efficiency.

¤ Documenting processes and training your team are the keys to unlocking your own time, as you'll be able to delegate more.

¤ Don't be afraid to automate these processes where possible.

16.
Changing the funding

Clients often come to us at different stages to help them obtain funding.

The first task is to calculate how much funding the client needs and when. This can be done through a fairly standard business plan, using some of the software I've mentioned in Chapter 3.

Factors in choosing finance

Once you know the amount and timing of the funding required, you can start to look at the alternatives. This is the initial checklist for deciding which type(s) of finance to recommend:

- What amount is needed.
- When it's needed. Funds required at short notice will always cost more, so the further ahead you can help your client to plan, the better. It may be possible to take on more-expensive short-term finance whilst you look for cheaper, long-term funding. This is also why you may need to prepare regular cash-flow forecasts for some of your clients where they need regular support to cover things such as salaries and VAT bills.
- How long the money will be needed for.
- When repayments will be made and how much.

- Any security available, such as property, equipment or invoices. These can be sold by the lender if the loan isn't repaid. Having available assets to provide security will reduce the cost of the finance.
- The (perceived) risk of the business. This will depend on things such as the nature of the business, the competence of the owners, previous borrowing and repayment, and the current trading and profitability. A riskier business will cost more to finance.
- Any other outstanding debts, as this will mean fewer resources available to repay the loan. A high debt-to-equity ratio makes it harder to raise finance.
- Other services required, such as the expertise of angel investors and venture capitalists.

Types of funding available

You may need to explain to your clients what different types of finance are available and which is the most suitable for their needs. Each type and its pros and cons are detailed in the following sections.

Grants

There are often grants available for specific reasons. If the business is investing in assets, coaching, training or creating jobs, there's usually some sort of funding. Grants don't need to be repaid, but the business may be required to match funding (i.e. to invest an equivalent amount). The local Chamber of Commerce is usually a good source of information on government grants.

Pros – No repayment is necessary.

Cons – It's limited to specific uses, and match funding may be required.

Personal savings

These are often seen as free, but there's an opportunity cost to the lender, as they could be generating income and earning interest elsewhere.

Pros – It's cheap.

Cons – Limited resources are available.

Family loans

These are usually easier to obtain if the owner has family or friends with resources, as they'll be investing in the owner as much as the business. All loans should be documented, and the terms of repayment and interest should be agreed in writing.

Pros – It's often cheap.

Cons – It may lead to disputes with family/friends if it isn't clearly documented and/or repaid.

Credit cards

These can be convenient for specific purchases or short-term funding when first setting up a business, but they're one of the most expensive forms of finance. They can be a good way of managing your short-term cash flow, as you'll have a month to make arrangements to pay them off or find replacement finance.

Pros – They're easy to obtain.

Cons – These are one of the most expensive ways to finance a business if not repaid in full within the month.

Bank overdraft

You may already have an overdraft facility that you can dip into for short-term finance. This will cost more than a bank loan, but it's much more flexible as you only pay for it when you need it.

Pros – This is easily accessible and flexible.

Cons – This is more expensive than a bank loan, and it may require a personal guarantee from the directors. It's usually repayable on demand.

Bank loans

These are fairly straightforward, but as decisions on these are often made by computer, rather than by experienced individuals, they may not be suitable for anything high risk or out of the ordinary. Your client will need to present a business plan that clearly shows how the loan will be repaid. Loans can be secured on assets such as property or equipment.

Pros – These are straightforward.

Cons – They're unsuitable for risky or complex requirements, and they may require a personal guarantee from the directors.

Asset finance

These are simple to obtain when purchasing assets, as there's clear security in the form of the asset itself.

Pros – These are straightforward.

Cons – They're secured on assets right up until the final penny has been paid.

Invoice finance

There are different ways of raising finance secured on your unpaid sales invoices. One way is to receive an advance on the outstanding debtor balance minus a finance charge, and another way consists of selling/assigning your debts to a collection company at a reduced value. Either method may require you to pay back any advance based on invoices that turn out to be irrecoverable bad debts. Invoice finance can be obtained through your bank, Satago or other sources.

> **Pros** – This is a relatively cheap source of finance, as the funds are secured on the invoices. For many service-based businesses, this may be their only asset for security.
>
> **Cons** – Invoices can only be raised once trading has started.

Peer-to-peer lending

Individual small investors pay into a group-lending scheme in return for a certain rate of return. The scheme then lends its money to small businesses, which repay the loan plus interest. Investors are often prepared to take a little more risk than banks, so it may be easier to obtain finance this way.

> **Pros** – It may be easier to gain than bank finance.
>
> **Cons** – Investors expect a higher rate of return.

Crowdfunding

Crowdfunding has become popular over recent years, but most projects fail to raise their target funding. To have the best chance of success, it helps to have the majority of cash promised before the official launch, which means lots of individual approaches before launching on the platform. Crowdfunding can be in exchange for early or discounted access to products, and there isn't usually any need to repay it.

> **Pros** – It creates an early audience for your product and isn't usually repayable.
>
> **Cons** – You need to generate a high take-up before the official funding launch date.

Share issue

Funds can be raised through issuing shares in the company. The equity won't need to be repaid in the same way as debt. This requires a knowledge of company law.

Pros – It doesn't need to be repaid.

Cons – It's complex. You need to generate sufficient interest, and it dilutes ownership of the company.

Angel investors and venture capitalists

There are many sources of this type of finance, and groups often arrange pitching events around the country. You can help your clients to prepare both their pitch and their business plan.

Funding may be in the form of debt, equity or a mixture of both. The funding often comes with regular reporting requirements, but it also provides access to expertise and useful introductions.

Pros – This provides access to expertise and/or introductions.

Cons – It engenders additional reporting requirements and other obligations.

Help finding funding

The good news is that there are several software platforms available to help find funding. This means you can search numerous resources at the touch of a button. Here's an outline of some of these platforms (see Appendix 1 for website details for the items listed):

- **iwoca** – This provides finance, and all applications are considered by an individual.
- **Capitalise and Swoop** – These offer access to numerous grants and loans through a single platform.

- **Chamber of Commerce** – Not a software platform, but your local Chamber of Commerce will have information on the latest grants available.

The type of finance that suits your client best will depend on the amount of money they require and the length of time that they wish to borrow it for. It's always easier and cheaper to get finance if they can offer security by way of assets, personal guarantees or share capital.

Identifying their cash needs early will give you time to shop around for the best deals and lower interest rates.

Summary

¤ Help your client to work out how much funding they require, when they need it, and how and when it'll be repaid, along with any interest.

¤ Advise your client on the best type of funding to meet their needs.

¤ Use finance platforms to help them to source finance faster.

¤ Prepare business plans and pitch packs for larger funding requests.

17.
Changing the tax

Tax advice is often referred to as business advice, but it really comes after the business planning. A business shouldn't be planned around the best tax advantages, but tax should be a consideration in every business decision. In other words, don't put the tax cart before the business horse.

You can easily minimise your annual tax by increasing your business costs. If you make no profit, then you'll pay no tax. Or you can legitimately stay below the VAT registration limit by stopping sales just before you reach the cut off. You just make less profit (although you will have time for a holiday, so it's not all bad news).

There's also the question of what's classed as tax advice? One friend was singing the praises of her accountant, who advised on whether they should incorporate and whether they should voluntarily VAT register. Whilst these things are clearly tax advice, they're things that we discuss freely in blogs, and our firm's app even includes a free incorporation calculator. So tax advice isn't just for the tax experts.

What other sorts of tax advice should generalists be giving? How about an onboarding and annual tax check? Here's my suggestion of questions to ask about your clients:

- Are they using the best trading vehicle?
- Are they on the best VAT scheme?

- Are they correctly claiming all the expenses they can, including home office, motor expenses and telephones?
- Are the director-shareholders taking money out of the business in the most tax-efficient way?
- Are they making the right level of pension contributions?
- Are they making all charitable contributions in a tax-efficient way?
- Does their spouse (if they have one) have any unused tax allowances that can be transferred?
- Are they only just above a marginal rate that can be mitigated by pension or charitable contributions?
- Are any company cars being bought in the most tax-efficient way?
- Should interest be paid on any loans to/from directors, and if so, at what rate?

*You can come up with more questions yourself,
depending on your knowledge of tax.*

There's then the more complex tax planning that can be identified by a generalist, but it may need input from a tax specialist to actually implement for items such as the following:

- Enterprise investment scheme (EIS) / seed enterprise investment scheme (SEIS) to encourage investment in the business
- R&D tax credits
- Patent box claims
- Inheritance tax planning
- Remuneration planning

A very good way to do this is to team up with a local tax adviser who can offer you regular tax reviews on some or all of your clients. They'll be in the best position to identify suitable plans to help your clients.

Alternatively, Diagnostax provides software to identify opportunities and also offers access to experts (for a monthly fee) to look after a set number of clients. It includes material to promote your tax services, and you have access to its tax panel or can use its experts to carry out any work necessary.

Don't forget that you should be looking out for tax planning opportunities in every conversation about business plans, as well as training your bookkeepers to spot anything too.

Advanced tax planning

This may be legal, but there's always the question as to whether it's moral. It's up to you whether you choose to offer this sort of advice.

Summary

- Speak to your clients regularly to see if there are any tax planning opportunities in their business plans.
- Spot prospects for tax planning in their bookkeeping.
- Carry out regular tax health checks when onboarding a client and at least once a year thereafter.
- Consider software for you tax health checks.
- If you aren't a tax expert yourself, then team up with a local tax adviser so that, between you, your clients will receive holistic care.

18.
Changing the value

If a client is looking to exit their business in the next five years, then they may need help to increase its value. There are several ways to do this, but they fall into two main categories:

1. Increase the income and profitability
2. Decrease the dependence on the current owner

Most of the other chapters will deal with ways to increase the profitability of the business, so this chapter will focus on reducing dependence on the business owner. Most business sales have some sort of handover period, if not an extended earn-out period, but the preparation should be based on the idea of handing over the keys and walking away.

Start with what happens when your client goes away on holiday. Do they need to take their laptop away with them? Do they take it "just in case"; "to keep an eye on my emails"; or because they need to do a little work each day?

What are the decisions and queries that make the business owner so essential?

What would happen if they were knocked over by a bus or succumbed to a pandemic?

Procedures

Start by documenting all the processes within the business. Make them as foolproof as possible so that any suitably qualified person can pick them up and follow the steps to complete the job. Procedures can't cover every eventuality, but start with the most common ones.

Training

Train the appropriate team member to carry out these processes and free up the owner. This may require bringing in additional resources. Whilst you're training one person, you can train a second person as back-up in case your first choice is ill or moves on to another organisation.

Alternative expertise

Sometimes, the owner is essential because they're the only one with that particular expertise. As always, there are ways of dealing with this, and the actual route may be a combination of them:

- » Train up somebody else within the organisation.
- » Recruit somebody with the expertise, either full time, part time or on a subcontract basis.
- » Retain an external expert. This is quite common in accountancy; for example, where small practitioners subscribe to a tax service or have an arrangement with an individual.
- » Document general knowledge. You don't need to be Samuel Pepys, but after a meeting with a customer or supplier, the owner should make notes on the key information gained and the decisions made. This can be

recorded on a customer relationship management (CRM) system.

» Get a locum in. An architect could have an arrangement with another local architect or somebody recently retired who could be on hand to answer technical questions if needed.

We see both of these last two suggestions in the medical profession. Doctors transfer patient notes between shifts, and treatment plans are documented for anybody to follow. In addition, locums may be brought in to cover absences and busy periods (e.g. in general practice).

Timesheets

Another way to start moving the owner out of the business is to see how they spend their time. Keeping approximate timesheets for a week or so will allow you to see what they're doing. It may be that they aren't actually doing anything that's essential to the business, so it's only ego that keeps them glued to their laptop on holiday. If this is the case, then you may need to be very diplomatic, or perhaps suggest that their partner or travelling companion takes charge of the laptop for the duration. Encourage them to feel proud of the way they've built a business that can work without them on a day-to-day basis. Explain that there's plenty of work to be done in developing the business further or in preparing for retirement.

Often, the owner is busy, but it's on tasks that can be done by somebody much more junior. I only have to look at my own business to see that I'm still doing my own bookkeeping and accounting "to keep my hand in". I'm not adding value to the organisation by messing around with simple things like this, but I reassure myself that "I can give it up any time I want to!" Business owners often hold on to jobs out of sentiment, and these are often the hardest to tear away from them.

Other jobs are easier to delegate if the benefits are clear. I write my own content each week, but I hand it over to my PA to turn it into two emails and two blogs for the different sides of my business. I was able to give this up because it takes a disproportionate amount of time and, quite frankly, it's dull. My PA then creates some lovely social media cards, which are much more creative than anything I could come up with. I was able to relinquish this because she does it better than me. I'm also quite comfortable being surrounded by people who are better than me at what they do.

Hobbies

Sometimes, the business owner is keeping themselves busy because they have no other hobbies. You may need to work with them to encourage them to take up a new hobby or to have a proper holiday, which will force them to take time out of the business.

If they can't be persuaded to take up a leisure pursuit, then there's always the mentoring route. Schools, universities and business organisations are always looking for experienced business people to volunteer their time and expertise to help youngsters or start-ups. Retirement may be the end of that business-knowledge acquisition, but it's a chance to share with others what they've learned.

Systemising, delegating and automating

We've already looked at this in Chapter 15.

What next?

Once the business owner has moved themselves out of the day-to-day work, they can focus on improving the business. They can still act as extra resource in busy periods or as sickness cover, but their role has now changed to working *on* the business, with time to implement or drive your advice forwards.

This can all carry on whilst they start the hunt for a buyer.

No fire sale

With a well-thought-out route to retirement, the owner can sell their business for the maximum value because, day to day, the business can clearly work well without them. They're improving and increasing the value of their business right up until the day they hand over the keys to the new owner. There's no desperate rush to sell, because the independence of the business means the owner can take time for holidays or hobbies, so they can ease into retirement at the right moment.

Summary

¤ You need to improve profitability whilst decreasing dependence on the owner.

¤ Find out what really happens when the owner is on holiday.

¤ Find out how the owner spends their time at work.

¤ Download the owner's knowledge into procedures and file notes.

¤ Find cover for the owner through training or bringing in access to expertise.

¤ Move the owner to focusing on working *on* the business.

¤ Encourage the owner to develop interests outside the business.

19.
Changing the marketing

People don't usually associate accountants with marketing advice, but it's important to be able to measure and evaluate the effectiveness of different marketing actions and campaigns. There will always be a delay between receiving/accessing marketing and action for some customers, but we should still be helping clients to track patterns and trends. There will also be some marketing that's purely – or partly – to raise awareness, and the effectiveness of this is much harder to measure. I'm trying to say that the true value of marketing exceeds what we can see just by measuring the immediate responses, so don't just ditch a campaign because there's no instant return.

But that's all about measuring historical numbers, and this book is about changing those numbers.

If you don't have marketing experience or expertise in-house, then this is an ideal time to partner with a local marketing strategist.

A good marketing strategy needs to attract the right sort of customers/work and to send a consistent message to those people. A message that will gradually bring them into a closer relationship with the business.

The business needs to be clear on who the right customers are and what the right sort of work is. This is why you should start by establishing the client's vison and values, as explained in Chapter 11.

Vision and values

The vision and values are unchanging, and marketing messages should always be in line with the values and move the business forwards towards the vision.

Branding

Branding is much more than having a pretty logo. It's the consistent message that a business sends out to its prospects (and everybody else) about who it is and what it stands for. The detailed messages may change at different stages of the journey, or when talking about different products or services, but the underlying brand should stand firm and be recognisable amongst this.

If a stranger tells us something, we're often cynical and evaluate both them and their message before deciding whether to act on it. When a friend gives us a tip, we already trust them, so we're likely to act much faster. It's the same if a stranger or a friend asks us for money; we'll often give or lend a reasonable amount of money to a friend without a second thought – sometimes, quite large amounts. This is because we know and trust that friendship.

Good marketing should build a similar trust in the business and the brand. So how can we help our clients to do this?

In the same way that you build any relationship, you can do good things in and around your core business. This can be basic quality and customer service (see Chapter 21) or through a reputation built on fair dealing and corporate social responsibility (CSR) (management speak for being a decent human being). Reputation is an important part of your brand.

A new or small business may build its brand around the owner, but in order to grow, there needs to be a similarly strong business brand.

We need to help our clients to pin down what they want people to think about when they see the logo or hear the brand name.

"They may forget what you said, but they'll never forget how you made them feel" – this has been attributed to Maya Angelou and others.

What are the three main things that prospects should feel when they're reminded of the business?, There are numerous branding exercises in other business books that you can do to help your clients identify these three things, and your marketing campaign should incorporate them at every step. In fact, your whole business should incorporate these, as they're much more than just a façade.

Ideal customer

As I write this book, I can picture you sitting there. I have a clear image in my head of who you are. In reality, you may not be that exact person, but if this book resonates with you, there's a fair chance that you have a lot in common with my client avatar.

Help your clients to establish their ideal client.

We use an ideal client form, which goes into all sorts of detail, including what TV programmes they're likely to watch, whether they have kids and what newspapers they read. Not because the business may be considering TV advertising, but because it's a way to make their client avatar come to life. We like the client avatar to have a name too.

Hunting niche vs trading niche

There's often confusion that marketing to a single type of client means you can't work with other types. This is nonsense. You need to be very specific in your marketing, so that you can build that resonance and connection in all your communications, as well as creating a product offering that will really attract them. But inevitably, there will be enquiries from other businesses too. For instance, I aim all my coaching marketing at accountants and yet, at the time of writing, about 50% of my coaching clients are accountants, 25% are bookkeepers and 25% are other business owners. One of my clients actively markets to Certified B Corporations (B-Corps), but they work with anybody with similar values.

The hunting niche is used for marketing. The business will almost certainly work with a broader range of clients. However, it may still choose to identify a niche for the work it does in order to provide a limited but expert service or to save having to stock every single item under the sun.

As well as helping your clients to decide on their hunting niche, they need to agree their trading niche. Even if they don't have a trading niche, there will be people that they don't want to work with. For instance, Hudson Accountants and Advisers didn't work with sole traders, start-ups or non-VAT-registered businesses. Our systems were all set up to deal with businesses of a certain size, and so we were too expensive for smaller businesses that didn't fit into our ideal. Instead, we provided free Money Matters events and cheap Xero training, as well as referrals to other accountants and bookkeepers.

Message at different stages

The message that businesses are sending out will vary at different stages, and it's often likened to dating:

- **Awareness** – Making sure that they know you exist. Perhaps friends will introduce you (or make a referral in business terms), or perhaps they'll just spot you in the right place at the right time? Of course, you'll present yourself in the best light, but there's no point in being deceptive, as you'll be found out at a later stage. In dating, if you post out-of-date or touched-up photographs on a dating site, you'll create a huge dissonance on that first meeting. The same goes for your marketing material; the message must be in keeping with what people will find when they get to know you a little better. If you run a small business, then there's no point trying to look like a big corporate. Instead, you can base your marketing message around the personal service that you're able to offer.

- **Interest** – A little conversation, but no commitment at this stage. Do you like each other enough for a date? Perhaps you've asked your friends about them or had a quick look at their social media? At this point, you're trying to establish if you have enough things in common to spend an evening together without yawning with boredom. We're not thinking marriage yet, just whether they want to spend a few hours in your company. Similarly, if somebody is interested in your business, they'll ask questions, and you'll be able to answer all of them. Build your messages around what people are likely to ask at this stage, and keep those messages short until they're interested in spending more time with you.

- **Testing the water** – A first date, with no pressure; you're both still on your best behaviour, and – hopefully – will have a nice time, but he/she may not be for you. Is there a cheap or low-cost way that people can sample the business's products or services before committing large amounts of cash to them? For my coaching business, I write books and articles, give talks, and have a discovery call. I don't want to force anybody to work with me if it's not right for them.

» **Relationship** – You hit things off and decide to invest in spending some time together. This is what we all aim for. And we work hard in that initial period to do things for the one that we care about, whether this is a partner or a client. The aim is to deepen that relationship so that they want to stay.

» **Marriage** – You have complete and utter loyalty to each other, but you still need to look after your partner and never take them for granted. In business, this is where the customer service comes in again. What's the business equivalent of red roses or breakfast in bed?

As you can imagine, producing the engagement ring at the awareness stage could be a little off-putting. Similarly, a lack of commitment at the marriage stage is a recipe for disaster. This is a gradual journey that may take some time. As an outsider, it's often easier to see the journey and to help your client map the route their own customers will take before falling head over heels in love.

Consistency

We all have both busy and quieter periods, but it's important that there's a consistent minimum level of marketing. Once your client has their marketing programme planned for the year, then they can delegate or outsource much of it, so that things still happen even when they're busy.

I create my own content each week, but my PA turns the words into e-newsletters, blogs on two sites, social media posts, etc. Look for ways to ensure that things can continue independently of the business owner. It's even possible to buy in content; I write monthly blog posts for accountants and occasional articles for fintechs, but if you aren't able to engage me, there are other copywriters available with accounting and business expertise.

Most things can be delegated to an expert who won't just save time but will do a far better job. Help your client to schedule a minimum level of marketing that they can sustain throughout the year. They can always do more in quiet periods, but they should never fall out of public view just because they're busy.

Lazy marketing

Okay, it's not really lazy, but it's efficient use of your marketing assets to reuse the material in as many ways as possible.

> We used to run quarterly Money Matters events at which I'd give a 20–30 minute talk on a topic related to business growth. Like many people, I hated public speaking at the time, and so I was determined to get the most out of each talk. For this talk, we used the content in all the ways listed in the *Video and photography* section in Chapter 11, plus we spoke about the talk in networking speed-dating introductions as an example of how we helped clients and others (rather than just telling people we were proactive).

If your client is using content marketing, then think about how every piece of content can be used to maximum effect.

What type of marketing to choose

There are many different types of marketing. There's push marketing, which reaches out to prospects, and pull marketing, which draws prospects towards the business. There's online or digital marketing, and there's offline marketing. There's so much to choose from, and experts in each and every field.

Once you have the marketing strategy in place for your client, it's time to make some introductions to your network of people who can implement the work. I recommend that you build up connections with the following:

- Marketing strategists
- Marketing coaches
- Graphic designers
- Artists
- Audio-visual experts for recording and editing webinars, podcasts and/or adverts
- Digital marketing experts who understand Google Ads, LinkedIn Ads and Facebook Ads
- Advertising experts for online and offline adverts
- Copywriters for content or just straplines
- Branding experts
- Website designers to handle the technology, visuals and search engine optimisation (SEO) of the written content (if required, they may engage professional copywriters on your behalf)
- Printers
- Networking groups
- LinkedIn experts (real ones, not just people who say they are)
- Influencer marketing agencies
- Events organisers
- And many more

Summary

When advising on marketing, do the following:

- ¤ Consider introducing one or more experts to your client.
- ¤ All marketing should be in line with the vision and values, so do the exercise to identify those first.
- ¤ Remember that branding is more than a logo.
- ¤ Build a client avatar to focus marketing on the right prospects.
- ¤ Agree the hunting niche for marketing and a broader trading niche for operating.
- ¤ Track the journey from awareness to dedication.
- ¤ Agree a minimum level of marketing that will always be conducted, even during busy periods.
- ¤ Reuse each piece of content in as many ways as possible.
- ¤ Build your network of marketing experts for advice and for implementation.

20.
Changing the sales

I'm never quite sure where marketing ends and sales begins. As with the roles of bookkeeper and accountant, the line between sales and marketing has blurred over time. For the purposes of this book, I'll talk about the marketing being up to the point of enquiry, and the sales will include the discovery call, the quote, the acceptance and the sign-up process. This may be because I'm more comfortable with the idea of marketing than sales, which can feel like a dirty word reminiscent of a less entertaining Del Boy Trotter.

I'm sure we've all been on the end of an overeager sales pitch. Not least from software providers that seem to mistake interest on behalf of a hypothetical future client for immediate buying signals. Or is it just me who likes to learn all about the latest tech, just in case I need it?

All this makes us fearful of being too pushy when we need to sell our own services. And if we can't do it for ourselves, how on earth can we advise our clients about sales?

We need to focus on the problems that we solve, because we're selling solutions to those problems. In exactly the same way that we sell the solution to our clients, we need to be confident because we've sold it to ourselves first. This is another opportunity for an external adviser to see things that the business owner can't. It'll also force them to explain this in a way that we, an outsider to their areas of business, can understand.

Selling is something that few accountants are good at, so it might seem odd to be training our clients to do this. This makes it ripe for outsourcing or providing advice in conjunction with The Gap or Phil Sayers of Proten Sales Development (see Appendix 1 for website details).

The Gap provides content, training and support to accountants to help them provide advisory services to their clients in sales and other areas. The content comes in the form of webinars and other marketing assets, as well as training and cue cards.

Proten Sales Development can provide one-to-one or group sales coaching. It specialises in working with accountants, but it will also advise your clients too.

The essential steps of a sales conversation are these:

1. Identify the problem or pain point.
2. Identify the solution.
3. Specify the outcome.
4. Explain the positives that have now replaced the pain.

This comprises the type of factual, logical work that accountants are usually good at, but we also have to use our emotional quotient (EQ) skills in order to understand how the problem causes pain and how the solution provides relief. As accountants, we're often not good at discussing emotions, but our non-accountant clients may find this much easier and might struggle to quantify the logical and financial benefits of their solutions.

The important thing is to open the conversation and to listen to what the prospect is saying, but also to work out what they're not saying. The problem they bring to you may not be the full picture, so ask questions until you're clear about the real issue from their answers.

All these things can help you to start a conversation. Here's an example:

Salesperson: If I've understood you correctly, you need help with [problem]; is that correct?

Prospect: Yes.

Salesperson: And is this a problem because of [reason]? Is this something that keeps you awake at night?

Prospect: [Confirms the consequence of the problem.]

Salesperson: What if we were able to improve it by [explains solution they sell and how it can help]? Would that solve the problem and help you sleep at night?

Prospect: Yes, it would.

The salesperson (you) can then start to discuss the options and pricing.

The call ends when a decision is made or a follow-up action is agreed. "No" is a perfectly valid decision.

If only all sales conversations went as smoothly as this example!

Your role is to help your client understand the problem(s) that their products or services solve. They need to understand how that impacts their customer financially and in other ways. They must then clarify how they will solve the problem. You can help your clients to develop scripts and rehearse these, and you can also assist with other training.

Depending on the business, the client may have a straightforward price list or they may need to prepare a quote for each sale. You can advise on the software they can use to generate these and how they should be followed up, at what point information is gathered for things such as credit control checks, and what other information needs to be collected at each stage and how that data is handled. Accounts need to be opened as quickly as possible to enable trading to begin, but certain checks still need to be undertaken.

As well as any legalities, there may need to be introductions to account managers, detailed orders and specifications, etc. All these need to be handled seamlessly from day one to manage the new customer's experience. The first 100 days of any new relationship are often considered the most important, and customer service should be built into every step.

Summary

- ¤ This is a key area for introducing other experts to your clients to advise them.
- ¤ Sales is about matching the solution to the client's problem, but only if it's the right solution.
- ¤ The first 100 days are crucial in any relationship.

21.
Changing customer services & quality

Sometimes, it's necessary to change customer service and quality as a remedial action because there's an issue that means the client is spending time, money and other resources resolving problems. But it's also a way to provide a service or product with a wow factor that will allow them to earn a premium above that charged by their competitors.

Once again, systems are often the key to this, in that we should find what works, and then be able to replicate it each and every time.

Cost of rework

There's often a financial cost to quality failures, which is made up of the following:

- Time and money to replace the product or redo the service.
- Time to manage the customer's complaint.
- Reputational damage, which is harder to measure (but that doesn't mean it doesn't exist).

If you're able to come up with some costs for this, then it'll be easier to convince the client to invest in improvements. You can then measure the impact of those changes so as to demonstrate the return on their investment.

A 1% improvement

Often, there are commercial pressures to get to market sooner than we might like with a product or service of minimum viability. But it's important that it isn't the end.

Quality is a continuous improvement process. Improving by just 1% per day is a 3,778% improvement over 365 days, or 1,329% if, like me, you prefer to keep weekends for non-business things.

You can probably spot a couple of big wins for each of your clients by walking through their processes as an objective outsider, but you can definitely identify lots of smaller wins that can be implemented quickly.

Customer service with a wow factor

Creating a wow is often adding a human touch to a well-automated process. Here are a few ideas, but you're ideally placed to view your clients objectively to recognise what they could easily do better.

Parking

Do they save the best parking spaces for the directors or for visitors? How about putting the visitor's name on a space rather than just "Visitor"? Can they go one step further and arrange for the car to be valeted during the meeting?

Welcome

Is their reception team well briefed to welcome visitors by name and to not misspell names on badges? Does the team put out a sign to welcome them? Do they keep a note of how their customers and contacts take their tea or coffee, and whether they prefer certain biscuits? Do they even provide biscuits?

Onboarding

Welcome gifts and cards are simple to organise, and they often make new clients feel valued, especially if there has been a lot of paperwork or upfront costs. It's very important to make the best impression during the first 100 days, so do they have a process for ensuring this?

Birthdays and anniversaries

If they have records of these, it's easy to arrange an appropriate card, gift or discount each year. Some restaurants are very good at sending discounts prior to customers' birthdays and anniversaries. Just make sure they have an appropriate General Data Protection Regulation (GDPR) policy to cover their use of this data.

Named contact

With everything being so automated these days, people often don't know who to contact if something isn't right. Can they provide a named contact? What about a welcome call from the contact, which can broadly follow a script?

Ease of contact

Too often, we're trying to avoid random contact to protect our time. Emails are sent from no-reply addresses, and there may not be a phone number or an email address on our website to reduce the hassle of bots trawling for contacts. There are a number of ways to manage this, even in a small business:

- **Webchat facility** – We use Melu on both the Hudson Business Advice and Minerva Accountants websites (see Appendix 1 for website details if you want a look). The chat is operated by real people who start with a list of FAQs and gradually build up more answers by searching your website or feedback on the call scripts.

- **VoIP number and an answering service** – You could use these services to filter your calls. We use Answer It, which is the same service we used for years at Hudson Business Accountants and Advisers. With the old business, they picked up calls that were diverted when our main lines were engaged or not answering. With the current business, the lines are permanently redirected to them. When using a VoIP number or landline, strangers don't have access to your mobile numbers.

- **Web forms** – These can be used in preference to giving email addresses.

- **Calendly.com** – This is a free service to use for booking meetings and calls; for those who don't have a PA to organise this for them, it can help you to avoid playing phone tennis. It's not personal, so take care with the wording on invitations, but it is convenient.

Useful information

A website should answer all the FAQs directly or make it easy to get in touch, as mentioned previously. When providing a service or product, it's important to keep customers informed of timescales, whether that's regarding the timings of deliveries or responses to queries, as appropriate to the business (e.g. Minerva Accountants aims to prepare accounts within eight weeks and to answer queries within one working day). These timescales sometimes form part of the formal contract, but on other occasions, they are just estimates, depending on the nature of the work. Domino's Pizza has a great tracking visual, but a simple autoresponder with an estimated timescale may be enough for small businesses.

Best practice

Feel free to borrow best practice and good ideas from another industry if they'll transfer well to your clients' sector. As accountants, we get to deal with so many businesses, and often across more than one industry, that we can pick up all sorts of good ideas to help our clients.

Summary

- ¤ Calculate the cost of poor-quality goods/services or rework.
- ¤ Focus on finding incremental improvements for your clients.
- ¤ Walk through their processes to see how they can improve quality or the customer experience.
- ¤ Borrow ideas from other industries.

22.
Changing the overheads

Changing the overheads is similar to financial control and is closely aligned with typical accountancy skills.

We can run all sorts of reports to assess the level of overheads vs previous periods or budgets, but what we really need to be doing is measuring, as far as possible, the return on the business's investment in these overhead costs.

Marketing effectiveness

It's always hard to assess how effective a company's marketing has been, as even if you ask prospects where they heard of the company, they often only mention one of several contacts. Marketing for general awareness is the hardest to assess.

As far as possible, we need to help our clients tie marketing costs to enquiries so that they can see what's most effective for them whilst also understanding that marketing is indeed a dark art.

Premises

Leasing or buying is a big decision when it comes to most assets, such as property, cars, machinery and even computers. Purchasing a premises through a self-invested personal pension (SIPP) can be quite tax efficient, but leaseholds and shorter-term rentals are more flexible.

Consider the size of your client's business and how fast they're growing. Will they fill a larger premises quickly, or will they be stuck in a building that's too big or too small for them? Serviced offices may cost more per square metre, but they provide much needed flexibility for changing businesses, as they can potentially just add to their lease an extra office in the same building without needing to change address or telecoms. Serviced offices also provide access to meeting rooms, reception services and other shared facilities.

You may need to help your clients to find the most appropriate premises for their business, as well as considering the working-from-home option. You may also need to advise them on the requirements for more remote working, both in terms of technology and how best to manage their team remotely.

Staff

When preparing a business plan, staffing is often a key issue. Additional sales people can generate more revenue, but they need to be supported by operations and other services.

You need to consider current and future staffing requirements, as well as succession planning. These roles can then be filled by full-time or part-time staff, outsourcing, or even automating part of some roles. As a sympathetic outsider, you're in a good position to advise on staffing issues without emotion.

What they get for their money

Go down every line of the profit-and-loss statement and review exactly what your clients are getting for their money. Question why they use particular suppliers. This is not just about pricing but also about particular services, efficiencies and ease of use.

When it comes to reducing costs, it's worth looking at Reducer software. Through a quick link to common bookkeeping software, Reducer can advise on cheaper pricing for things such as utilities, and it can even take into account such requirements as green energy and other environmental credentials. Once agreed with the business owner, Reducer can organise the switch, and its costs are covered by the supplier.

Impact of spending more

As well as looking for reductions, consider the impact of spending more. For each cost, look at any benefits that might result from doubling expenditure. Investing in marketing or sales personnel might speed up growth, but investing in automation might improve efficiency or reduce costs elsewhere.

Summary

- ¤ Look at spending vs both budget and prior periods.
- ¤ Advise on alternatives, such as lease vs buy options.
- ¤ Look at switching suppliers.
- ¤ Consider spending more for better results.

23.
Changing the rest

There are so many areas that our clients need help with, and we're their main – perhaps only – professional adviser. Here are some ideas of other areas that might suit your expertise.

Wealth management

Some accountants are also qualified as independent financial advisers (IFAs) because there's an opportunity to offer both when working with high-net-worth individuals. Many IFAs already offer generous commissions to accountants, which must be disclosed to the client. Many accountants are wary of compromising both their independence and their reputation for trustworthy advice and referrals by accepting commissions. In this case, it might be more valuable to rely on cross-referrals.

IFAs do a lot of forecasting of personal income requirements as well as investment growth. My own IFA uses software and some very basic assumptions to do this, so it won't surprise you that these forecasts are much less sophisticated than my own personal ones. This is an area where accountants excel. Many IFAs are focused on investments as a retirement plan, but we deal with business owners who often have a saleable business to take into account and perhaps some investment property. This means we have a more holistic approach than many IFAs.

With the increased visibility of IFA fees and increased regulation pushing these fees up, there's a gap at the bottom end of the market. All in Place (formerly Tether) software can be used to provide client forecasts and advice through accountants holding a designated professional body (DPB) licence.

Mortgage advice

This is a regulated area, so it's probably safest and easiest to partner with a reputable mortgage adviser or business.

Human resources (HR)

There's the whole field of HR that our clients need help with. Membership of the FSB includes access to some standard legal templates, employment law advice and tax advice. These templates are very useful to start with, but as a business grows, they may need to be tailored to the specific needs of the business, due to it having a larger number of staff and some more-senior/more-expensive employees, which justifies those staff having individual contracts. Any businesses with staff will almost certainly need help with the following at some point:

- Recruitment
- Employment contracts
- Employment handbooks
- Disciplinary processes
- Personality profiling
- Appraisals
- Staff development

- Team building
- Employment tribunals

If you offer payroll services, you may well be asked questions about any of these areas.

There are all sorts of local experts on the legal and HR sides, but you could also partner with Citrus HR software and services, plus Joanne Wharam of Smart Support for Business (see Appendix 1 for website details).

Legal services

Every business needs legal services. As mentioned already, membership of the FSB includes access to some standard legal templates, employment law advice and tax advice.

You may have local legal experts you could work with, or you could use a service such as Lawbite.

Businesses will usually need the following at some point:

- Company secretarial services
- Incorporation with bespoke articles of association
- A shareholder or partnership contract
- Terms and conditions of sale
- Credit control follow-up
- Employment contracts
- Mergers and acquisitions contracts
- Leasehold or freehold property contracts

They may also need help bringing or defending more litigious matters.

Mergers and acquisitions

The work around such large transactions might involve a number of experts as well as providing initial advice. It could include the following:

- Business valuations
- Advice on integrating multiple businesses (i.e. systems and processes)
- Legal advice and contracts
- Tax advice
- How to structure the deal legally, financially and in a tax-efficient way
- Funding acquisitions
- Raising capital
- HR issues and Transfer of Undertakings (Protection of Employment) (TUPE) when staff are involved
- Property expertise
- Intellectual property, trademarks and patents

Insurance

This is a regulated area, so it's probably easiest to partner with a reputable business or adviser. The sorts of insurance that your client may need are these:

- Public liability
- Professional liability
- Employer liability
- Cover for stock, cash, goods in transit and other assets
- Bad-debt cover
- Key-person cover

- Life assurance
- Private health insurance
- Motor insurance
- Travel insurance
- Tax-investigation cover

Succession planning

Running a sustainable business necessitates that it isn't dependent on any one individual. We've looked at systems and procedures elsewhere in this book, but there also needs to be a back-up person for each role. They may only be required to step up temporarily to cover sickness or holiday, or it may be longer term to replace an employee who has moved on. A growing business needs to develop the next person for each role in order to promote those they need to free up for higher or more expanded roles.

Environmental concerns

This is an area that's perfect for accountants to get involved in. My first exposure was as an environmental auditor about 20 years ago, but there's more scope than just this.

We can measure and assess a business's current environmental status, help with complex legislation, advise on changes and improvements, and measure the results of these actions.

Whilst this might be enough for small businesses, we can partner with experts for larger or more complex organisations.

Cybersecurity

Whilst we can give some general advice in this area, it's probably more suited to us partnering with an expert. If you have your own in-house IT team, it may be able to provide this for your clients too.

Quality

Whilst we can give some general advice in this area, it's probably more suited to us partnering with an expert.

Health and safety

Whilst we can give some general advice in this area, it's probably more suited to us partnering with an expert.

As you can see, there are all sorts of areas where your clients may be looking for help. Decide what you want (and are able) to do in-house and where you need to introduce experts to your clients.

Summary

Other areas where you may be able to help your clients are as follows:

- Wealth management
- Mortgage advice
- HR
- Legal services
- Mergers and acquisitions
- Insurance
- Succession planning
- Environmental
- Cybersecurity
- Quality
- Health and safety

Closing thoughts

In the first part of this book, I discussed how to set up and offer advisory services to new and existing clients. Their success will lead to your success. There should be sufficient information in this book to get you started on your advisory journey, if you haven't done it before. I've also given ideas on how to scale up your advisory services if you're currently the only person in your organisation able to help clients in this way.

Take the ideas and adapt them to suit yourself and your own way of working. All businesses deserve the very best advice we can give them.

The second part of the book details some of the specific advice that you can provide for clients in a number of areas. This isn't a comprehensive list of advice or the areas that you can help in, but I'd like to think that it's a good starting point for beginning or expanding your advisory services.

I'd suggest you read some or all of the books listed in Appendix 2 for further advice you can give to your clients, but the more you read and research, the more ideas you'll have available at your fingertips.

If it hasn't been clear throughout this book, I'm passionate about helping businesses to thrive and the part that accountants can play in making this happen.

Please connect with me on social media for more current ideas:

Twitter: @DellaHudsonFCA

LinkedIn: Della Hudson FCA

Sign up for our weekly Top Tips for Accountants *and* Better Business *webinars via our website: www.hudsonbusiness.co.uk*

Please share stories of your successes and how you've helped your clients with their success.

References

Gerber, M.E. (2001). *The e-myth revisited: Why most small businesses don't work and what to do about it.* New York, NY: Harper Business.

Ferriss, T. (2011). *The 4-hour work week: Escape the 9–5, live anywhere and join the new rich.* London, UK: Vermilion.

Hudson, D. (2020). *Growing by numbers: How to scale up your small business with confidence.* Bristol, UK: SRA Books.

Moran, B.P. and Lennington, M. (2013). *The 12-week year: Get more done in 12 weeks than others do in 12 months.* Hoboken, NJ: Wiley.

Michalowicz, M. (2017). *Profit first: Transform your business from a cash-eating monster to a money-making machine.* London, UK: Portfolio.

Appendix 1
Software & resources

The software mentioned in this book is constantly being updated and new features added all the time. There's also new software being introduced. The following are links to the software mentioned in the book, which I've used and like. Their inclusion in this book is based on my personal preference and not due to any sponsorship.

It isn't intended to be a comprehensive software review, as there are plenty of other apps that I haven't mentioned. Where possible, I've asked the software companies to check what I've written for accuracy, but my primary purpose is to reflect on how you can use the software to advise your clients, rather than to promote any particular app.

The best way to stay up to date is to subscribe to these:

App Advisory Plus - appadvisoryplus.com

BlueHub - bluehub.co.uk

Or sign up for our regular webinars at hudsonbusiness.co.uk/accountants.

Chapter 2

The following software can help to optimise your historical data.

Data entry

AutoEntry - www.autoentry.com

Dext Prepare (Receipt Bank) - dext.com/uk

Expensify - www.expensify.com

Flux - www.tryflux.com

Hubdoc - www.hubdoc.com

rise.global - www.rise.global

Till software

Clover – www.clover.com

Payment software

GoCardless – gocardless.com

Stripe – stripe.com/gb

PayPal – www.paypal.com/uk/home

Amazon-compatible software

A2X – www.a2xaccounting.com

Web shops

Shopify – www.shopify.co.uk

Bookkeeping software

FreeAgent – www.freeagent.com

QuickBooks Online (QBO) – quickbooks.intuit.com/uk

Sage – www.sage.com/en-gb

Xero – www.xero.com/uk

Bookkeeping checks

Syft Analytics – www.syftanalytics.com

Xavier (Dext Precision) – xavier-analytics.com

Recording training videos

Loom – www.loom.com

Group advisory programmes for affordability

Growing by Numbers Online (this can be white labelled for you and your clients) – hudsonbusiness.co.uk/business-owners/

The Numbers Business Online – hudsonbusiness.co.uk/accountants

The ScaleUp Blueprint – hudsonbusiness.co.uk/accountants

Chapter 3

Pre-advisory software for management accounts and forecasting

Fathom - www.fathomhq.com

Fluidly - fluidly.com

Float - floatapp.com

FreeAgent - www.freeagent.com

Futrli - www.futrli.com

QuickBooks Online (QBO) - quickbooks.intuit.com/uk

Sage - www.sage.com/en-gb

Senta - www.senta.co/gb

Syft Analytics - www.syftanalytics.com

Xero - www.xero.com/uk

Chapter 4

Presentation skills and speaker coaching

Alexandra Bond Burnett - www.speakingambition.com/about

Scott Johnston - www.scottjohnston.net

Personality profiling and teams coaching

Joanne Wharam at Smart Support for Business - www.smartsupportforbusiness.co.uk/about-us

Advisory software to help you start or scale

Capitalise - capitalise.com

Clarity - clarity-hq.com

Fathom - www.fathomhq.com

Satago - www.satago.com

Senta - www.senta.co/gb

Chapter 5

The following can help with making your accountancy business a role model.

Online courses

The Numbers Business Online - hudsonbusiness.co.uk/accountants

The ScaleUp Blueprint - hudsonbusiness.co.uk/accountants

Practice Management software to improve the smooth running of your business

AccountancyManager - www.accountancymanager.co.uk

Pixie - www.usepixie.com

Senta - www.senta.co/gb

For help with pricing and onboarding

Go Proposal - goproposal.com

Practice Ignition - www.ignitionapp.com

Chapter 6

Webinars

Minerva Accountants' *Money Matters* - minervaaccountants.co.uk/webinars

Chapter 7

Software to help sell advisory services

Clarity - clarity-hq.com

Third-party resources for group or individual advice sessions

Entrepreneurs Circle - entrepreneurscircle.org

Growing by Numbers Online - hudsonbusiness.co.uk/business-owners/

The Gap - www.thegapportal.com

Webinars

> Minerva Accountants' *Money Matters* – minervaaccountants.co.uk/ webinars

Chapter 8

For information on dual branding copies of *Growing by Numbers* to promote your advisory services to your clients, then please do get in touch (hello@hudsonbusiness.co.uk). You can also add your own foreword if you prefer.

Chapter 9

Some of the third parties you can use to help provide business advice to your clients

> Action Coach – actioncoach.co.uk
>
> Entrepreneurs Circle – entrepreneurscircle.org
>
> Growing by Numbers Online (this can be white labelled or a simple referral) – hudsonbusiness.co.uk/business-owners/
>
> Hudson Business Accountants and Advisers (advice coaches) – hudsonbusiness.co.uk/accountants
>
> Local coaches

Chapter 10

Writing a book

> Alexa Whitten at The Book Refinery – www.thebookrefinery.com
>
> Sue Richardson at The Right Book Company – www.therightbookcompany.com

Improving your speaking skills

> Alexandra Bond Burnett at Speaking Ambition – www.speakingambition.com/about
>
> Professional Speaking Association – www.thepsa.co.uk

Scott Johnston – www.scottjohnston.net

Toastmasters – www.toastmasters.org

Promoting you and your events

PR the Write Way – prthewriteway.co.uk

Webinars

Hudson Business Advice's *Better Business* – hudsonbusiness.co.uk/accountants

Minerva Accountants' *Money Matters* – minervaaccountants.co.uk/webinars

Chapter 12

For help with terms and conditions

Federation of Small Businesses (FSB) – www.fsb.org.uk

Simply-Docs – simply-docs.co.uk

For help with improving cash balances

Chaser – www.chaserhq.com

GoCardless – gocardless.com

iwocaPay – www.iwoca.co.uk

Satago – www.satago.com

Square – squareup.com/gb/en

Stripe – stripe.com/gb

Zettle by PayPal – www.zettle.com/gb

Chapter 14

For help with DiSC profiling, managing teams and conducting appraisals

Smart Support for Business – www.smartsupportforbusiness.co.uk/about-us

Chapter 15

We (Hudson Business Advice - hudsonbusiness.co.uk/business-owners/) can provide coaching, training and retreats for business owners.

Chapter 16

Funding platforms

Capitalise - capitalise.com

iwoca - www.iwoca.co.uk

Swoop - swoopfunding.com

Invoice financing

Satago - www.satago.com

Chapter 17

Tax advice service

Diagnostax - www.diagnostax.co.uk

Chapter 20

Sales training

Proten Sales Development - protensd.co.uk

The Gap - www.thegapportal.com

Chapter 21

Example websites using online chat

Hudson Business Advice - hudsonbusiness.co.uk/accountants

Melu (web chat) - meluchat.com

Minerva Accountants - minervaaccountants.co.uk

Chapter 22

Software for reducing costs and swapping providers

Reducer – reducer.co.uk

Chapter 23

Other contacts to help improve your client's business

All in Place (formerly Tether) (investment support) – www.allin.place

Citrus HR (HR software and support) – citrushr.com

Federation of Small Businesses (FSB) (legal templates and support) – www.fsb.org.uk

Joanne Wharam at Smart Support for Business – teams support www.smartsupportforbusiness.co.uk/about-us

Lawbite (legal support) – www.lawbite.co.uk

Appendix 2
Business books

Introduction

Hudson, D. (2018). *The numbers business: How to grow a successful cloud accountancy practice*. Bristol, UK: SRA Books.

Chapter 2

Hudson, D. (2018). *The numbers business: How to grow a successful cloud accountancy practice*. Bristol, UK: SRA Books.

Hudson, D. (2020). *Growing by numbers: How to scale up your small business with confidence*. Bristol, UK: SRA Books.

Gerber, M.E. (2001). *The e-myth revisited: Why most small businesses don't work and what to do about it*. New York, NY: Harper Business.

Thomas, B. (2020). *Watertight marketing: The proven process for seriously scalable sales*. s.l.: Human Business Thinking.

Chapter 5

Hudson, D. (2018). *The numbers business: How to grow a successful cloud accountancy practice*. Bristol, UK: SRA Books.

Hudson, D. (2020). *Growing by numbers: How to scale up your small business with confidence*. Bristol, UK: SRA Books.

Chapter 8

Gerber, M.E. (2001). *The e-myth revisited: Why most small businesses don't work and what to do about it*. New York, NY: Harper Business.

Ferriss, T. (2011). *The 4-hour work week: Escape the 9-5, live anywhere and join the new rich*. London, UK: Vermilion.

Hudson, D. (2020). *Growing by numbers: How to scale up your small business with confidence.* Bristol, UK: SRA Books.

Moran, B.P. and Lennington, M. (2013). *The 12-week year: Get more done in 12 Weeks than others do in 12 months.* Hoboken, NJ: Wiley.

Michalowicz, M. (2017). *Profit first: Transform your business from a cash-eating monster to a money-making machine.* London, UK: Portfolio.

Chapter 10

Hudson, D. (2020). *Growing by numbers: How to scale up your small business with confidence.* Bristol, UK: SRA Books.

Richardson, S. (2106). *The Authority Guide to Publishing Your Business Book: Take your business to a new level by becoming an authority in your field.* Bristol, UK: SRA Books.

Whitten, A. (2018). *Publish Your Way to More Clients: How to plan, write and publish your book so that you are 'The One' in the eyes of your potential customers.* Portsmouth, UK. Compass-Publishing.

About the author

Della Hudson has been working in accountancy since 1989 when she first started training as a chartered accountant after completing her degree in chemistry and management at City, University of London. Apart from a brief spell in IT, she spent most of her career working in industry and helping to run UK subsidiaries of large multinationals.

In 2009, whilst she had two small children, Della set up her own chartered accountancy practice – Hudson Business Accountants and Advisers – working from her kitchen table. She grew it to a team of eight people in independent offices before selling up in 2018.

With no thoughts of retiring, Della now works as a speaker, writer and business coach to all sorts of businesses, alongside running her second practice – Minerva Accountants. Her first book, *The Numbers Business: How to grow a successful cloud accountancy practice*, won the specialist book category at the 2019 Business Book Awards, and it became an Amazon bestseller. Her second book, *Growing by Numbers: How to scale up your small business with confidence*, was written to help accountants start advisory conversations with their clients. She then went on to co-author the Bloomsbury book *Tax Planning 2019/20*, finally impressing her then teenage kids by sharing the same publisher as their beloved J.K. Rowling. Della was even shortlisted as the Institute of Certified Bookkeepers' personality of the year in 2019, which is quite an achievement for a Hufflepuff!

In her free time, Della enjoys the swim-bike-run of triathlons, cooking and eating with friends.

With thanks

Thank you to all the other accountants and fintechs who gave up their time to be interviewed for this book.

This work was inspired by Senta, resulting from a desire to help accountants offer advisory services to its clients, so the marketing team at Senta commissioned me to write a 2,000-word guide on the subject. Whilst scoping out the guide, I realised I had a lot more to share, and so this book was conceived.

Even before that, I'm not sure whether any of my books would have been more than a daydream if Rebecca Cave and Accountingweb hadn't started me on the path to becoming a professional writer back in 2017. Thank you for your support throughout my career(s), starting with including me in the Class of 2009 and everything since.

Della

Printed in Great Britain
by Amazon

25341004R00118